Successful Faculty Development And Evaluation:

The Complete Teaching Portfolio

by John P. Murray

ASHE-ERIC Higher Education Report No. 8, 1995

Publication Date: 1997

Prepared by

Clearinghouse on Higher Education
The George Washington University

In cooperation with

Association for the Study
of Higher Education

Published by

Graduate School of Education and Human Development
The George Washington University

Jonathan D. Fife, Series Editor

Cite as

Murray, John P. 1995. *Successful Faculty Development and Evaluation: The Complete Teaching Portfolio.* ASHE-ERIC Higher Education Report No. 8. Washington, D.C.: The George Washington University, Graduate School of Education and Human Development.

Library of Congress Catalog Card Number 9679498
ISSN 0884-0040
ISBN 1-878380-74-5

Managing Editor: Lynne J. Scott
Manuscript Editor: Barbara Fishel/Editech
Cover Design by Michael David Brown, Rockville, Maryland

The ERIC Clearinghouse on Higher Education invites individuals to submit proposals for writing monographs for the *ASHE-ERIC Higher Education Report* series. Proposals must include:
1. A detailed manuscript proposal of not more than five pages.
2. A chapter-by-chapter outline.
3. A 75-word summary to be used by several review committees for the initial screening and rating of each proposal.
4. A vita and a writing sample.

ERIC **Clearinghouse on Higher Education**
Graduate School of Education and Human Development
The George Washington University
One Dupont Circle, Suite 630
Washington, DC 20036-1183

This publication was prepared partially with funding from the Office of Education Research and Improvement, U.S. Department of Education, under contract no. ED RR-93-002008. The opinions expressed in this report do not necessarily reflect the positions or policies of OERI or the Department.

EXECUTIVE SUMMARY

New York Governor George Pataki says of SUNY faculty in the *Rochester Democrat and Chronicle*'s Labor Day edition: "I think they can get more productivity out of the workforce." The story makes it clear that Pataki is talking about more hours in the classroom, which he believes translates into better learning for students. The newspaper story also notes that Ohio recently passed a law requiring college and university teachers to spend 10 percent more time in the classroom. The sponsor of that law says: "Universities and colleges kind of consider themselves above it all, . . . where us common folk can't really comprehend what they do. . . . With tuition rising at a tremendous rate, there's got to be some rules."

Much of this type of criticism is based on misconceptions that teaching involves only the time spent in the classroom and that professors spend very little time teaching. Educators must demonstrate that the hours spent in the classroom are only part of the real work of teaching. One means to this end is the teaching portfolio, which can provide professors with a vehicle to document the *quality* and *quantity* of their teaching.

What Is a Teaching Portfolio?
Teaching portfolios can be defined in at least four ways by focusing on their purpose. First, teaching portfolios are vehicles for documenting teaching, with the emphasis on demonstrating excellence (see, e.g., O'Neil and Wright 1992). Second, teaching portfolios are vehicles that empower professors to gain dominion over their professional lives (see, e.g., Seldin 1991). Third, teaching portfolios are vehicles to provide institutions of higher learning with the means to demonstrate that teaching is an institutional priority (see, e.g., Braskamp and Ory 1994). Fourth, teaching portfolios are vehicles for individualizing faculty development (see, e.g., Seldin 1993b; Shore et al. 1986).

What Does Higher Education Value?
The introduction of teaching portfolios requires institutions to critically examine what they value, and what institutions value is ultimately reflected in their reward structure. Unfortunately, four-year colleges and universities on the whole reward research. Until this situation is changed, in actions as well as in words, teaching will always take a distant second

place to publications, grants, and the other public marks of the researcher. "[It] is futile to talk about improving the quality of teaching if, in the end, faculty are not given recognition for the time they spend with students" (Boyer 1990, p. xi). A critical first step to recognizing and rewarding good teaching is to develop effective ways to assess teaching performance.

The appraisal of performance must be individualized for it to ultimately affect teaching (Blackburn and Pitney 1988). But "individualization in teaching is threatened by the typical way it is assessed, namely, by student evaluations. . . . They establish a uniform set of standards and assume that certain behaviors are good and [that] the absence of those behaviors constitutes proof of poor teaching" (p. 32). Student evaluations appear to have little impact on the improvement of teaching, however (Ory 1991), and something more is needed if colleges and universities are serious in their desire to improve teaching through performance appraisal. "A portfolio system would accomplish the goal of continuous growth and development, the realization of the individual's full potential" (Blackburn and Pitney 1988, p. 32).

What Should a Teaching Portfolio Contain?

Most portfolios incorporate a statement of the professor's philosophical beliefs about teaching and learning. Philosophical beliefs shape, sometimes in subtle ways, human behavior. When professors reflect on how a particular reading, a specific teaching style, or a particular assignment relates to their philosophy of education, they are examining deeply held convictions. Therefore, much of the remainder of the portfolio details how professors put their beliefs into practice in and out of the classroom. Most important, much of the portfolio should be devoted to reflection on how behaviors are congruent with beliefs. Most portfolios also incorporate a plan for altering behaviors found to be incongruent with the professor's philosophical assumptions about teaching and learning. And the portfolio should incorporate a strategy to assess the appropriateness and success of the new behaviors.

How Can Administrators Build Interest?

Building interest ultimately means managing change—in this case, a significant change in the culture of higher education.

Administrators need to become effective change agents. Because of our socialization in graduate education, most of us are well steeped in the "traditions" of academe; therefore, it can be quite challenging to guide others through changes seeking to radically alter that hegemony. If the change is to be significant and lasting, administrators should develop methods to include most faculty in the process—not simply in the product. For many administrators, it means learning more about how to implement change, garner support, and overcome resistance.

If the improvement of teaching and learning is the ultimate goal of a portfolio project, most faculty will want to learn how to assess the effectiveness of their teaching and students' learning. Although the literature on faculty evaluation has included references to formative evaluation for some time, these references usually fail to include advice on how one might go about this vital task of assessment. Although many faculty are quite capable of knowing when students are not understanding the material, often professors do not know how to go about discovering *why* students are not learning. Therefore, the complete portfolio project should plan activities intended to help faculty *learn how* to assess their teaching, their students' learning, and the currency of their courses.

The difference between a faculty evaluation system that supports faculty and one that demoralizes faculty can be found in the care that goes into designing a *systematic and comprehensive* evaluation system. Evaluation is effective when administrators and faculty work together to develop the instruments and procedures rather than when administrators impose them on the faculty. Administrators and faculty working together should start by determining the purpose(s) of evaluation, who will be evaluated, how often, who will do the evaluating, and, most important, what will be evaluated.

Department chairs should take great pains to publicly connect the outcomes of faculty evaluation to the reward system. When the faculty evaluation process demonstrates that an individual is a good teacher, chairs must be certain that the institution rewards the individual. For too long, rewards have gone solely to the faculty who excel at research. Teaching portfolios can provide an effective means of recognizing good teaching. And the recognition of good teaching is the first step toward adequately rewarding it.

CONTENTS

FOREWORD

"Colleges and universities do not place enough emphasis on good teaching!" The number of times that critics of higher education repeat this thought in newspaper articles, popular magazines, and speeches indicates that, to a great number of people, this thought contains a great deal of truth. Supporting this belief is the result of recent surveys of faculty indicating that the majority believe research and publishing are more highly valued and rewarded than teaching. On the other hand, college and university leaders insist that quality teaching is their institutions' most important activity. But if it is, why does the opposite perception still persist? The answer is that both perceptions are accurate and inaccurate—mainly because all parties concerned have ignored several fundamental realities.

Several fundamental conditions of human behavior must be observed if an organizational culture is to change.

- *The law of reward and appreciation.* People move in the direction where they perceive they are most rewarded and appreciated for their actions.
- *The law of survival.* People adjust their actions according to how they perceive those actions affect or improve their ability to survive.
- *The law of value.* Because teaching is often protected by the cloak of academic freedom, it is most often conducted without direct observation other than by the teacher and the students. Research publications and conference presentations, however, are more often conducted in public and are easily seen and counted.
- *The law of legitimate measurement.* For measurement to have an impact, a consensus must be reached on the accuracy or legitimacy of that measurement. Because of the difficulty in measuring it, the academic profession has not developed a consensus on how to define and measure "quality teaching."

By ignoring these laws of human behavior, institutions continue to articulate their belief in quality teaching but have rewarded faculty for activities more easily measured—which, more often than not, emphasize research and publishing. According to one wag, it is a perfect example of insanity: doing the same thing, the same way, every time, but expecting different results.

Some institutions have searched for ways to do things differently that would more successfully change the culture and increase their emphasis on teaching. One technique has been the implementation of teaching portfolios. According to John P. Murray, assistant professor of educational administration at SUNY–Brockport, the teaching portfolio takes into consideration some of the fundamental laws of human behavior: It collects tangible evidence of a faculty member's teaching activities, it creates a focal point to examine and evaluate past teaching, and it sets specific goals for future teaching activities and performance. Through its use over time, the portfolio can develop a record of teaching quality and improvement that can successfully compete against the measurable qualities of research and publishing. The use of the teaching portfolio helps to create greater appreciation and reward for an individual's teaching, reinforces and promotes greater effort toward quality teaching, and therefore becomes a self-reinforcing process toward the promotion of quality teaching.

Ernest Boyer, in *Scholarship Reconsidered: The Priorities of the Professorate* (1990), speaks to the importance of recognizing the scholarship of teaching. This respect for teaching as a scholarly activity will never reach parity with publishing or conference presentations until teaching becomes more visible and more measurable. The use of teaching portfolios can be one method to help increase a focus on the quality and scholarship of teaching and help develop tangible evidence that will help give teaching the same respect and rewards that are given to other forms of academic scholarship.

Jonathan D. Fife
Series Editor,
Professor of Higher Education Administration, and
Director, ERIC Clearinghouse on Higher Education

ACKNOWLEDGMENTS

This monograph could not have been completed with the support of my wife and colleague, Dr. Judy I. Murray. Her encouragement and willingness to forgo other activities so I could finish this work is greatly appreciated. She also proofread every part of the book numerous times, catching countless careless errors. Despite her efforts, I am quite certain some errors still remain, for which I accept full responsibility.

I am also indebted to Dr. Anthony F. Grasha at the University of Cincinnati, who conducted a professional development workshop that was the source of the idea for this work.

INTRODUCTION

This monograph is about how teaching portfolios can improve the quality of teaching and learning in higher education. Teaching portfolios are a means to improve the state of teaching in higher education because they provide educators with the scholarly opportunity to study and reflect on the teaching and learning processes. Before teaching portfolios or any other innovation can take root in higher education, however, the prevailing culture of higher education institutions must be examined and perhaps altered (Shelton and DeZure 1993).

Higher education is increasingly under siege. Critics openly question whether higher education serves its students, and many claim that higher education has lost its focus on its mission (Dillon and Lieberman 1996; Gardiner 1994; Lucas 1996; Shelton and DeZure 1993). Some critics are forming powerful alliances with lawmakers, who are withholding funding and demanding faculty teach more students and more classes and spend more time on campus and in the classroom. According to a January 1996 story in *The Chronicle of Higher Education,* 21 states have enacted legislation regulating faculty workloads.

The debate has even reached the national level. The chair of the U.S. House Committee on Children, Youth, and Families, Rep. Patricia Schroeder, authored a report in 1992 that states, "When it comes to a college education, American families are paying more and getting less, largely because the average professor is making $63,000 a year for teaching six to eight hours a week" (quoted in Schoenfeld 1992).

While many of these responses seem punitive and dysfunctional to educators, they require a response from educational leaders. Most educators, however, either do not respond or claim that the criticisms are based on misperceptions and are therefore invalid. The debate over the validity of the criticism may go on interminably within the ivied walls, but it seems clear that the public wants action now and its elected officials are responding. This failure of educational leaders to respond effectively only fuels the critics' attacks and legislative actions. In New York State, for example, the lack of effective leadership in the SUNY system has led to significantly decreased funding, increased tuition, increased control by elected officials, and the resignation of a chancellor. A few educational leaders are belatedly coming to the "recognition . . . that higher education must change, and, as in other sectors of society, repeated and insistent calls have been made for significant, even radical, reinvention, redefinition, and restructuring of our industry" (Gardiner 1994, p. 145).

To formulate a clear and decisive response, leaders in higher education must increase their awareness of the depth and breadth of the problem. Clearly, public and legislative criticisms center on the perceived lack of importance placed on teaching and the perceived poor quality of much teaching. Are these criticisms valid? Unfortunately, most colleges and universities cannot answer these criticisms. They simply do not have the data. Colleges and universities are just now beginning to assess learning outcomes (Gardiner 1994). Assessing educational outcomes, however, requires that we have an understanding of what they should be, and we do not. Assessing the quality of teaching requires that we have an understanding of what effective teaching practices are, and we do not.

The truth of the matter is that many teachers could improve. The good news is that most want to improve. Why, then, do we not find teachers working toward becoming better teachers? Chief among the varied causes usually offered is that teaching is not valued. If we consider only financial compensation, there is considerable truth to this allegation, but it is only part of the story. Of equal importance is that most professors are ill-trained to be teachers.

> *Trained only in the technical subtleties of literary, historical, or scientific research and in many cases cloistered in libraries or laboratories for years during their graduate training, they may never have read and reflected on the great classics of American liberal education and the history of the American college and university, studied the research illuminating their students' developmental psychology, learned the theory and practice of modern developmental academic advising, read the influential contemporary critical reports on higher education, or studied and practiced under supervision the design and implementation of modern instruction. Cast adrift in the profession without chart or oar by their graduate school mentors and new colleagues and lacking the perspective, personal philosophy, and basic educational skills requisite for*

*professional competence, new faculty sink or swim in
the classroom and advising conference to the enormous
detriment of their students and society* (Gardiner 1994,
pp. 142–43).

When searching for causes for the alleged poor state of
higher education, it would be easy to oversimplify. While it is
easy to place the blame on reward structures that favor research, publications, and grantsmanship over teaching and
the inadequate teacher training that professors receive from
graduate schools, the problems of higher education have several causes—not the least of which are the widely accepted
myths regarding the relationship of the professoriat to the
task of teaching that form part of the cultural hegemony of
higher education. "Improving college teaching and elevating
its status will require changes in the prevailing culture of the
academy, a culture that has become rigidly entrenched and
resistant to efforts to modify it. Long-term answers involve
systemic changes in our institutional culture" (Shelton and
DeZure 1993, p. 28). Systemic change in higher education
requires a significant cultural paradigm shift, and for this
change to occur, educational leaders will need to tackle four
myths that are deeply embedded in the culture of higher
education. Unless these myths are challenged, any attempt to
improve the quality of instruction by the introduction of
teaching portfolios is likely to fail.

*Myth #1: All
that is re-
quired to be a
good teacher
is a thorough
knowledge of
the discipline.*

- *Myth #1:* All that is required to be a good teacher is a
  thorough knowledge of the discipline.
- *Myth #2:* How to teach effectively cannot be taught; you
  either have it or you don't.
- *Myth #3:* Effective teaching strategies are generic and
  cross all disciplines.
- *Myth #4:* Effective teaching can be measured with a
  generic set of criteria. A corollary to this myth is that
  input from students is sufficient to assess the quality of
  teaching.

Regarding the first myth, most college teachers are well
educated in their specific discipline or, more often, in a narrow subset of that discipline. Although knowledge of one's
discipline is a necessary condition, it is not sufficient for
effective teaching. If it were sufficient, most college and

university teachers would be outstanding teachers. Despite evidence to the contrary, many college and university teachers and administrators clearly believe that knowledge of the material is all that it takes to teach effectively. While knowing the subject matter is important, effective teaching also involves knowing how to relate the material to diverse groups of students and understanding how to apply the material and methods to a wide variety of settings. At the present time, few opportunities exist for professors to engage *actively* in learning about teaching. The creation of a teaching portfolio would provide such an opportunity.

Concerning the second myth, the belief that teaching is an inborn ability or talent that cannot be taught or learned is somewhat bizarre when one considers that higher education institutions are in the business of teaching any other skill imaginable. To accept this widespread belief is to ignore the burgeoning body of research into cognitive psychology and how humans learn. Rather than thinking of a teacher as an artist with innate talent, it is more productive to think of a teacher as a craftsperson. Craftspeople may have raw talent, but they also need to perfect technique for the talent to show through. Until a craftsperson develops technique, any innate talent is likely to be quite useless. In other words, although some individuals may find it easier than others to be effective teachers, to be effective requires diligent effort. Individuals *can* learn how to teach better, even already good teachers, by diligent study of the teaching and learning processes. The creation of a teaching portfolio would provide such an opportunity.

Like most myths, the belief that effective teaching strategies cross all disciplines contains a small grain of truth. The ways in which disciplines approach their subject matter differ significantly, however, and those differences are reflected in teaching strategies. This "pedagogy of substance" (Shulman 1993) represents two distinct yet equally important images regarding effective teaching. The first is that effective teaching requires instructors to "know what will be readily understood by students, what will require extra time, and what will require a variety of instructional strategies to be understood and integrated by different types of learners" (Shelton and DeZure 1993, p. 37). For Shulman, this knowledge is the "wisdom of practice" and requires a comprehension of the triangular relationship among students, teacher, and subject matter. The second image is that professors tend to look to others within their own discipline for what they value and respect. If teaching is to truly matter, "we need to make the review, examination, and support of teaching the responsibility of the disciplinary community" (Shulman 1993, p. 6). The creation of a teaching portfolio would provide such an opportunity.

A corollary to the myth that effective teaching can be measured with a generic set of criteria is that students' input is sufficient to assess the quality of teaching. This myth, perhaps the most invidious of these four, causes colleges and universities to develop assessment instruments that speak only to a very general set of behaviors that are common across all disciplines. Typical teacher evaluation instruments for use by students measure teachers' behaviors, such as being on time, speaking clearly, being organized, providing clear objectives, and giving prompt feedback. Although these conditions are often necessary for effective teaching, they are *not* sufficient. A professor can, for example, provide prompt feedback that is of no assistance to a student, make clear objectives that should not be part of a particular course, and say it all with great clarity. The assessment of teaching requires that professors probe deeper than these standardized forms allow. "When faculty and administrators allow student ratings to be the only real source of information about teaching, they unwittingly contribute to a system in which too much emphasis is placed on evaluating superficial teaching skills and not enough is placed on more substantive matters" (Keig and Waggoner 1994, p. 1). Effective evaluation of teaching requires that the entire context of the teaching and learning equation be studied. The creation of a teaching portfolio would provide such an opportunity.

The culture of higher education will change significantly if teaching and learning are to occupy their rightful place at the center of the higher education mission. The study of teaching and learning will gain the same respect that other disciplines have enjoyed. Assessment of the effectiveness of teaching must be broadened beyond evaluations by students, and innovative and meaningful ways to assess teaching and learning will be needed. Professors will need to be shown ways of examining and reflecting on teaching and learning. "Too few teachers have examined in a systematic way how they teach or have thought about it seriously or reflectively" (Keig and Waggoner 1994, p. 7). But "improving college teaching should not be a model for remediation; it should be a model of ongoing improvement for all faculty, something shared with colleagues, and something reinforced throughout the learning community" (Shelton and DeZure 1993, p. 30). It is the contention of this monograph that teaching portfolios can satisfy this requirement.

The successful use of teaching portfolios, however, requires a substantial change in the prevailing cultures of higher education. And such changes will not be successful or sustainable without effective departmental leadership. Leadership must come from department chairs for several reasons, chief of which is that departments are the power base of all colleges and universities. Former Stanford University president Donald Kennedy argued that central administrators are relatively powerless to effect change "because the action is all peripheral: it takes place at the level of department faculties" (quoted in Zlotkowski 1996, p. 3).

Moreover, the failure of the generic approaches to improving teaching can be traced to the fact that they have ignored the importance of disciplinary differences housed in academic departments. These disciplinary differences largely disappear when efforts to improve teaching start with the department. "We need to reconnect teaching to the disciplines. . . . Like it or not, the forms of scholarship that are seen as intellectual work in the disciplines are going to be valued more than the forms of scholarship (like teaching) that are seen as nondisciplinary" (Shulman 1993, p. 6). When the talk of improving teaching comes from the central administration or a center for teaching and learning, faculty rarely relate. "Why? The conversation offered them remains too distanced from the intellectual excitement and challenge faculty feel working in their disciplines. The conversations proceed as through it didn't matter what was being taught or to whom" (Rhem 1991, p. 2).

The next five sections provide operational definitions and examples of how professors, colleges, and universities use portfolios; suggestions for the content of a teaching portfolio and how to organize it; suggestions for how colleges and universities can evaluate the quality of teaching by using teaching portfolios; examples of techniques that professors can use to gather data about their teaching and their students' learning; and a discussion about how higher education institutions might define effective or good teaching. The two sections after them provide, respectively, an analysis of the elements of organizational culture that will inhibit the successful introduction of teaching portfolios and some of the cultural conditions that need to exist for teaching portfolios to flourish, and the strategies department chairs can use to make teaching portfolios work in their departments.

WHAT IS A TEACHING PORTFOLIO?

One of the benefits derived from a teaching portfolio is the flexibility it provides individual faculty members, departments, and colleges. Consequently, a simple descriptive definition of the teaching portfolio would be somewhat undesirable. "Rather than settle on any fixed view of what 'it' is, . . . campuses [should] explore the many images of what portfolios might be" (Edgerton, Hutchings, and Quinlan 1991, p. 4). Moreover, portfolios are "intensely personal documents that take on the character of the owner" (J.P. Murray 1995b, p. 164). Therefore, operational definitions that focus on purpose provide the best definitions.

Operational Definitions

Teaching portfolios can be defined operationally in at least four ways by focusing on their purpose. They can be defined as vehicles for:

- Documenting teaching, with the emphasis on demonstrating excellence.
- Empowering professors to gain dominion over their professional lives.
- Providing institutions of higher learning with the means to demonstrate that teaching is an institutional priority.
- Individualizing faculty development.

Documenting teaching

When defining the teaching portfolio, most authors tend to emphasize that portfolios are vehicles for documenting a professor's teaching.

- *The goal of a teaching portfolio is to describe, through documentation over an extended period of time, the full range of your abilities as a college teacher* (Urbach 1992, p. 71).
- *The teaching [portfolio] is a comprehensive record of teaching activities and accomplishments drawn up by the professor* (O'Neil and Wright 1992, p. 6).
- *[The teaching portfolio is] a document that a faculty member creates to communicate teaching goals, to summarize accomplishments, and to convey the quality of teaching* (Waterman, quoted in Millis 1991, p. 217).

Moreover, many authors stress the ability of the teaching portfolio to illustrate what is best about a professor's teaching.

- *[A teaching portfolio] focuses on the characteristics of exemplary teaching and the best way to document and display them* (Millis 1991, p. 217).
- *[A teaching portfolio] is a factual description of a professor's major strengths and teaching achievements. It describes documents and materials [that] collectively suggest the scope and quality of a professor's teaching performance. It is to teaching what lists of publications, grants, and honors are to research and scholarship* (Seldin 1991, p. 3).
- *A teaching portfolio is a collection of documents that represent the best of one's teaching and provides one with the occasion to reflect on his/her teaching with the same intensity professors devote to their research* (J.P. Murray 1994b, p. 34).

Some argue that the concept of a portfolio should be expanded to include all the traditional aspects of a professor's work (Braskamp and Ory 1994; Centra 1993; Froh, Gray, and Lambert 1993). A faculty portfolio is "a comprehensive presentation of the works, activities, and achievements of faculty in the primary areas of the academy—teaching, scholarly activities, and services. [It is] a holistic portrayal of a person's professional capabilities" (De Fillips 1993, p. 11).

In the attempt to develop a more inclusive portfolio, however, the danger exists that teaching will once again be eclipsed by accomplishments in research. "For teaching to become important again, reputations built on publishing, scholarship, and research grants will have to be recast to showcase teaching" (Meacham 1993, p. 45). The real power of the portfolio resides in its potential to place teaching at the forefront of higher education.

Empowering professors

A second major thread running through the definitions of teaching portfolio is its potential to allow *individual* instructors to document "both the complexity and the individuality of good teaching" (Seldin 1991, p. xi). Portfolios afford faculty the "opportunity to define how they want to develop and assess pedagogical skills, command of subject matter, and professional skills" (J.P. Murray 1994a, p. 1).

- *The portfolio developer decides what goes into the portfolio. He/she states his/her teaching philosophy, how that is to be put into action, what the proper student outcomes should be, and, most [important], what standards of success he/she will be judged against. The teacher becomes the professional educator that standardized evaluation often militates against* (J.P. Murray 1994b, p. 36).
- *[The teaching portfolio] could encourage faculty to focus specifically on self-selected instructional variables as they prepared their materials. Through the process of establishing goals and selecting evidence to document [that] these goals had been met, faculty would be encouraged to improve their teaching as well as to verify current effectiveness* (Fayne 1991, pp. 4–5).
- *The teaching portfolio is a tool for examining the concrete evidence of one's teaching and reflecting on what it says about one's teaching and the student's learning. . . . The process of introspection used in the development of a portfolio enables faculty to reflect upon and assess their teaching practices against their values and beliefs and to communicate teaching accomplishments to others* ("The Teaching Portfolio" 1994, p. 1).
- *Teaching portfolios can have a special power to involve faculty in reflection on their own practice* (Edgerton, Hutchings, and Quinlan 1991, p. 6).
- *The portfolio process empowers faculty to access and improve their performance. . . . Empowered faculty feel: (1) driven to teach well because of intrinsic motivation rather than chair evaluations, and (2) that their teaching performance is primarily in their own hands* (Shulman and Rhodes 1995, p. 1).

The real power of the portfolio resides in its potential to place teaching at the forefront of higher education.

Demonstrating teaching as an institutional priority

The third major theme in the definitions of teaching portfolios revolves around their ability to emphasize teaching as an institutional priority. When a campus encourages its faculty to develop teaching portfolios, the entire campus engages in "a dynamic process [that], at the institutional level, opens campus dialogue on academic excellence" (De Fillips 1993, p. 11).

While colleges and universities often intend to use portfolios to emphasize the importance of teaching and learning, many soon recognize the portfolio's value for faculty development (Braskamp and Ory 1994). "While many institutions initially adopted and promoted portfolios to gather more evidence to increase the status of teaching on their campuses, many institutions now conclude that its greatest potential may be in the area of faculty development" (p. 231).

Individualizing faculty development
The fourth theme found in the definitions of teaching portfolios stresses, in fact, their potential to motivate faculty development.

- *[The portfolio is] a carefully assembled collection of "work samples" and reflective comment [that] has emerged as an effective vehicle for faculty to document what they know and do as teachers, while also promoting individual reflection and improvement* ("Use of Faculty Portfolios" 1993, p. 4).
- *[The portfolio] is a gathering of documents and other materials highlighting the professor's classroom teaching and suggesting its scope and quality. . . . It is flexible enough to be used . . . to provide stimulus and structure for self-reflection about teaching areas in need of improvement* (Seldin 1993b, p. xi).
- *The course portfolio begins the process of improvement by engaging in the scholarship of teaching, a strategy of critical inquiry into teaching performance in a single course, a starting point for better teaching all around* (Zubizarreta 1995, p. 3).

One author found the value of developing a portfolio in its requirement to identify and challenge his basic assumptions about teaching and learning.

> *Careful and rigorous introspection in asking oneself "why do I do what I do in my teaching function?" is essential. As I considered this question and others, I found my focus turning to issues of student learning. That is, I found my teaching was based on models I had constructed from observations of the best teachers from my past. My assumption was that if those models of teaching were effective for my learning, those same models would be effective for my students. In fact, one of the most important functions . . . is to continually*

remind the preparer to challenge implicit assumptions
that have developed over many years of teaching (Perry
1993, p. 16).

In reality, teaching portfolios are all of the above. They
are a means to document teaching, to showcase excellence
in teaching, to emphasize that teaching is paramount to the
mission of higher education, and to motivate faculty development. "Properly done, the portfolio will provide an accurate picture of a faculty member's current accomplishments
and status, as well as plans for improvement. . . . The quality of thought and effort one brings to the teaching enterprise will be revealed" (Perry 1993, p. 17).

These themes, however, do reveal a creative tension
among the various reasons offered for encouraging faculty
to develop a teaching portfolio. The notions that portfolios
should be manifestations of the institutional importance
placed on teaching and displays of one's best work seem-
ingly conflict with the notion that they are documents for
personal and professional development. On the surface, it
would seem that the room needed to reflect on one's teaching—room to experiment and to fail—is not found within
the definitions that stress showcasing good teaching. In fact,
two distinct varieties of portfolios could be emerging from
the literature.

One emphasizes the portfolio as a file, box, or dossier
that portrays "best" work, defined as ideal, flawless
performance. The second sees the portfolio as an expla-
nation and argument related to tough teaching chal-
lenges [and] goals [that] reflect[s] experimentation,
failures, and successes. . . . [It] includes . . . pedagogical
reasoning—the "thinking behind" the teaching perfor-
mance (Braskamp and Ory 1994, pp. 228–29).

Yet the apparent conflict among these strands is more illu-
sory than real. Because teaching portfolios "provide a connection to the contexts and personal histories of real teaching and make it possible to document the unfolding of both
teaching and learning over time" (Wolf 1991, p. 129), they
can serve diverse purposes.

The resolution of this apparent conflict can be found in
the determination of how the portfolio is to be used. "A

faculty member preparing a portfolio for review by a tenure committee might design a portfolio that looks quite different from one designed by a faculty member who is simply interested in taking a hard look at his or her teaching" (J.P. Murray 1994b, p. 38). Faculty need, however, to ascertain how the teaching portfolio is to be used before sharing it with administrators or colleagues. A faculty member who assumes that the portfolio will be used to improve teaching may willingly reveal weaknesses that would harm his or her chances to gain merit pay, tenure, or promotion. Penalizing a faculty member for honest reflection would be a sure way to destroy the spirit of cooperation needed for the use of portfolios to succeed on campus.

Why Teaching Portfolios?

By the beginning of the 1990s, between 50 and 75 campuses had implemented teaching portfolios (Seldin and Annis 1990, p. 197); five years later, 750 colleges were using them (Seldin 1995). The reasons for this phenomenal growth are many: "(a) it is cost-effective; (b) it is rooted in the context of discipline-related teaching; (c) it debunks the myth that effective teaching cannot be documented; (d) it gives faculty ownership of the portfolio process, building on intrinsic motivation; and (e) it capitalizes on the power of constructive consultation to generate meaningful change" (Millis 1991, p. 217). In addition:

1. Portfolios capture the complexities of teaching.
2. Portfolios place the responsibility for evaluating teaching in the hands of faculty.
3. Portfolios can prompt more reflective practice and improvement.
4. Portfolios can foster a culture of teaching and new discourse about it (Edgerton, Hutchings, and Quinlan 1991).

Putting a teaching portfolio together can result in several outcomes. Portfolios can assist a professor to:

1. *Identify specific duties of a course and how such responsibilities fit into the professor's teaching load and other assignments;*
2. *Articulate a philosophy for a particular course;*

3. *Describe, analyze, and evaluate course materials, meth-*
   ods, and outcomes;
4. *Examine course objectives and competencies;*
5. *Study student and peer reviews and formulate an action*
   plan for improvement;
6. *Posit specific teaching goals;*
7. *Provide supportive documentation of performance*
   (Zubizarreta 1995, p. 3).

The authors of these publications tout the ability of portfolios to place the responsibility for assessing and improving teaching in the hands of the faculty. Teaching portfolios derive their potency from this ability to place control in the hands of professionals. Teachers can define themselves in ways that show their individuality, the richness of their teaching, and the values that guide their teaching. "A portfolio also embodies an attitude that assessment is dynamic and that the richest portrayals of teacher (and student) performance are based on multiple sources of evidence collected over time in authentic settings" (Wolf 1991, p. 130). At the same time, faculty can clearly connect with the specific traditions and missions of their disciplines and institutions. In other words, teaching portfolios allow one to capture the depth and richness of teaching in ways that standard, computer-generated and -scored forms cannot.

Uses for Teaching Portfolios

Although educators came somewhat late to the concept of portfolios compared to other professionals, suggestions for their potential use are numerous. Four uses are possible from the perspective of the faculty member:

1. Receiving credit for effective teaching
2. Improving teaching performance
3. Receiving awards or merit pay for outstanding teaching
4. Obtaining a different position (Seldin 1991).

Several authors (Braskamp and Ory 1994; Centra 1993; Froh, Gray, and Lambert 1993) advocate the use of portfolios throughout a professor's entire career. Table 1 suggests that portfolios can be used in different ways at different times in one's career.

TABLE 1

Scholars' Use of Portfolios at Various Stages In the Academic Career

Stage	Purpose of Portfolio
Early Graduate School	Stimulate the collection of artifacts pertaining to teaching and research
	Promote reflection about initial teaching and other professional experiences
	Encourage discussion about professional activities with faculty mentors
Late Graduate School	Stimulate thinking about a philosophy of teaching and a future research agenda
	Assist in the academic job hunt
Pretenure Years	Facilitate promotion review
	Facilitate tenure review
	Encourage discussion about professional growth with colleagues, department chairs, and deans
Post-tenure Years	Encourage reflection about professional growth throughout one's academic career

Source: Adapted from Froh, Gray, and Lambert 1993, p. 105

Summary

Teaching portfolios are best defined operationally—that is, according to their intended purpose. Portfolios have been used to document teaching with an emphasis on demonstrating excellence, to empower professors to gain dominion over their professional lives, to provide colleges and universities with the means to demonstrate that teaching is an institutional priority, and to individualize faculty development. Undoubtedly, academics will use portfolios in all these ways and others not yet conceived; however, the two fundamental uses of portfolios are for the improvement of teaching and for personnel decisions.

Within these two purposes are the seeds of a potential conflict. "When portfolios are used for personnel decisions, the portfolio maker may be penalized for honest reflection on perceived weaknesses. In most personnel procedures, faculty need to emulate their students and attempt to hide their weaknesses from the judgmental authorities" (J.P. Murray 1994b, pp. 37–38). But the conflict need not occur if one determines the purpose of the portfolio before beginning to develop it. Clearly, a portfolio developed for the improvement of teaching will look quite different from one developed to win promotion, tenure, or merit pay.

What does all this mean for the teacher? Fundamentally, teaching portfolios provide faculty with the opportunity to display their teaching abilities and accomplishments. Simply documenting one's teaching, however, would neither justify the effort required to put a portfolio together nor unleash its powerful potential to improve one's teaching. The power of a portfolio is its ability to allow a professor to reflect on the true task of education—teaching.

WHAT GOES INTO A TEACHING PORTFOLIO?

The content of a teaching portfolio depends largely on its intended use, with the two most frequent uses to make personnel decisions and to improve teaching. Although both are legitimate purposes, a genuine tension exists between the summative and formative uses for teaching portfolios. While many (Blackburn and Pitney 1988; Centra 1993; Edgerton, Hutchings, and Quinlan 1991; Seldin 1991) believe both functions are compatible, others have reservations, fearing that

> . . . when portfolios are used for personnel decisions, the portfolio owner will be penalized for honest reflection on perceived weaknesses. . . . The complexity of this dilemma revolves around the implicit promise that compiling a portfolio will improve the quality of instruction. Presenting only one's best work would hardly occasion reflection on needed changes in one's teaching. Yet, when the stakes are high (e.g., tenure), revealing one's own imperfections becomes risky business (J.P. Murray 1994b, p. 38).

Although an anonymous reviewer of this monograph suggested that this fear is overstated, the danger exists that those skilled at creating the appearance of quality when it does not exist could deceive promotion and tenure committees. Not all academics have polished communication skills, and some faculty believe that a colleague has gained a promotion or tenure by turning in a "pretty but empty package." The same anonymous reviewer noted, however, that the solution to this dilemma is to require portfolios that are to be used in promotion and tenure decisions to conform to the same standards. These standards would include the required contents, the order of presentation, the maximum size the portfolio can be, what documentation must be included in the appendices, and so on.

Planning the Portfolio
First questions
Regardless of whether a portfolio will be used for summative or formative purposes, professors must answer some fundamental questions about its scope and breadth. Should the portfolio contain representative samples or only examples of one's best work? Will the portfolio contain everything or only representative artifacts of what one has compiled for

a course or term? Should it contain reflections on what the artifacts say about a faculty member's teaching? The consensus is that "the well-developed portfolio presents selected information" (Seldin 1992, p. 14) and "written reflections on the significance of the artifacts and events of classroom life" (Wolf 1991, p. 131).

An unorganized collection of artifacts is unlikely to provide insights into a professor's beliefs about teaching. Even selected documents and artifacts are unlikely to yield insights into how belief permeates practice unless the faculty member reflects on what they mean and how the artifacts demonstrate what faculty believe about teaching and learning. A mere collection of reflective essays is likely to "place greater emphasis on what teachers say they do in their classrooms than on what they actually do" (Wolf 1991, p. 132). Thus, a useful portfolio would be an organized set of artifacts generated during the process of teaching and reflections on how the artifacts reflect the scope and quality of a professor's teaching.

Organizing principles

Before one can decide what actually goes into a portfolio, one must decide how to organize it. To provide a coherent and meaningful view of a faculty member's teaching, a portfolio needs to have an appropriate layout for presenting the data and reflections. The organizational pattern depends on how the teaching portfolio is to be used and the needs of the faculty member. If the teaching portfolio is to be used for formative purposes, the content and organization should be flexible. If the portfolio is to become part of the data used for a summative evaluation, however, the organizational pattern and content should be standardized across the institution.

Several means of organizing teaching portfolios have been suggested. For example, a portfolio organized

> . . . around a theme extracted from one's philosophy of education and one's basic beliefs about the learning and teaching process becomes a thematic document that can prompt reflection on how one's teaching choices match one's beliefs about teaching. The emphasis is on fusing our beliefs about the learning/teaching process with methods, outcomes, and evaluation (J.P. Murray 1994b, p. 38).

Faculty members should

. . . assemble those artifacts of their lives that demonstrate where they have been and what has been accomplished. The faculty member would then draw up a plan of where he or she wants to go in both the short run and over the long haul, both being subject to alteration, especially the latter, as time passes. Next a faculty member would delineate what is needed to get from her or his current stage to the next one and what will constitute evidence that the new stage has been reached (Blackburn and Pitney 1988, p. 33).

The first organizing principle calls for a deep, thorough assessment of both a teacher's belief system and practices to see how well they match, the second for an assessment of past practice that can be used to improve the future. Thus, a portfolio becomes more than a "container into which many different ideas can be poured" (Edgerton, Hutchings, and Quinlan 1991, p. 4). A common thread will be woven through their diverse content. Teaching portfolios will all address what the portfolio owner believes is critical to teaching *his or her* students well. The thread will be woven throughout a reflective dialogue—both internal and external—about who, why, and what we are teaching. The process of developing a portfolio will force the professor to reflect not only on what he or she teaches, but also on *why* he or she teaches.

These organizing principles are somewhat abstract and philosophical and may need to be made a bit more concrete and practical for some faculty members. On the more practical side, the artifacts could be organized around their three sources: (1) materials from oneself, (2) materials from others, and (3) the products of good teaching (Seldin 1991, 1993b; Shore et al. 1986). The materials could be sorted into four sections.

The first part would comprise a collection of materials that demonstrate what the faculty member has been doing and what she or he has accomplished in teaching . . . during the evaluation period. The second part would be a plan outlining the faculty member's goals and specific objectives for the next evaluation period as well as a more general explanation of plans for the long term. In part three, the faculty member would describe

> ***The first organizing principle calls for a deep, thorough assessment of both a teacher's belief system and practices to see how well they match, the second for an assessment of past practice that can be used to improve the future.***

the kinds of support that he or she will need to reach short- and long-term goals. The fourth part would describe the evidence that demonstrates these goals have been reached (Hart 1989, pp. 2–3).

A portfolio could also be arranged around the following seven dimensions:

1. What you teach;
2. How you teach;
3. Change in your teaching;
4. Rigor in your academic standards;
5. Students' impressions of your teaching and their learning;
6. Your efforts to develop your teaching skills;
7. Assessments of your teaching by colleagues (Urbach 1992).

Yet another suggestion centers the teaching portfolio around six themes:

1. What one teaches;
2. Whom one teaches;
3. Why one teaches them;
4. How one's philosophy of education influences the design of courses and the choice of teaching strategies;
5. An assessment of one's effectiveness as a teacher; and
6. A plan for improving one's effectiveness (J.P. Murray 1995b).

These four suggested configurations can all be used profitably to organize one's artifacts and reflections. To be future oriented, however, teaching portfolios need to include a section on plans to improve one's teaching (Hart 1989; J.P. Murray 1995b).

Content
After the faculty member decides on an organizational design, the next question is what to include. Although the purpose for writing the teaching portfolio might dictate the content if improvement of one's teaching is the ultimate goal, some items are more effective than others (see table 2).

Tables 3, 4, and 5 present more detailed suggestions about what items might be included in a portfolio. The actual con-

TABLE 2

The Effectiveness of Items in a Portfolio for the Improvement of Teaching

Especially Effective
- Representative course syllabi
- Statement of teaching responsibilities and brief description of the way each course was taught and why
- Student ratings
- Description of curricular revisions, including new course projects, materials, class assignments

Somewhat Effective
- Students' scores on pre- and postcourse examinations
- A discussion of teaching goals for the next five years
- Statements from colleagues who have observed the professor in the classroom
- A videotape of the professor teaching a typical class

Less Effective
- A statement by the department chair assessing the professor's teaching contribution to the department
- A record of students who succeed in advanced study
- Statements by alumni on the quality of instruction

Source: Seldin 1995.

tent, however, should depend to a great extent on the person creating it and his or her purpose. These three tables are only general lists of what might be included, not what must be included, but faculty should recognize which items might give a more favorable impression of teaching competence and which might better be used for self-evaluation and improvement. The portfolio should be compiled to make the best possible case for effective teaching (Shore et al. 1986).

Parts of a Typical Portfolio
The table of contents for a typical teaching portfolio might look like the following:

1. Philosophy of education—assumptions about how learning takes place;
2. Statement of teaching responsibilities;
3. General goals;
4. The match between teaching strategies selected and philosophy and general goals;

TABLE 3

Items for Possible Inclusion in a Teaching Portfolio

What Is Taught

- List of courses taught
- Description of grading standards
- Reflections on the goals of each course—that is, is the emphasis on content or critical thinking skills?

Who Is Taught

- Students' characteristics (majors or nonmajors, lower division, upper division, graduate)
- Students' learning styles
- Motivation for taking the course

Why They Are Taught

- Students' goals
- Institutional mission related to course goals
- Departmental goals
- A statement of the essential content of the course—that is, a list of cognitive knowledge, skills, and/or attitudes

Documentation of Teaching Strategies

- Examples of assignments and exams
- Techniques used to assess students' learning styles
- Course materials prepared for students
- A list of teaching strategies used
- A statement about how assignments and exams reflect the faculty member's goals
- Classroom research techniques used to assess students' learning

5. Documentation of teaching effectiveness/reflection;
6. Summary of outcomes from previous renewal plans (if this is not the first portfolio);
7. A renewal plan, based on information gained during the process of compiling the portfolio.

Philosophy of education

The only essential component of the teaching portfolio is a

Assessment of Teaching Effectiveness

- Pre- and post-test scores
- Student evaluations
- Notes or other testimonials from students or former students
- Interview/survey data from students who have completed the class
- When the course is a prerequisite, statements from those who teach the following course(s)
- Teaching awards won
- Reports from students' employers
- Review of video/audio tapes
- Scores on standardized national or departmental exams
- Annotated copies of representative graded papers, projects, and exams
- Statements from colleagues who have visited classes
- Statements from colleagues who have reviewed syllabi and course materials
- Statements from alumni
- Statements from administrators who have visited the professor's classes

Teaching Improvement Plan

- Student evaluations from a previous term compared to a current term
- A list of readings on improving teaching and changes resulting from reflection on them
- A record of changes that result from self-reflection
- A record of on-campus faculty development activities attended
- Contributions to professional journals that deal with teaching improvement
- A description of new teaching strategies tried

Source: J.P. Murray 1995b, p. 171.

statement of what the author believes about teaching and learning. It has been called a philosophy of teaching or education (J.P. Murray 1994b, 1995b; O'Neil and Wright 1992), a "framing statement" (De Fillips 1993), and a self-assessment or reflective statement of teaching goals (Braskamp and Ory 1994; Davis 1993; Froh, Gray, and Lambert 1993).

Whatever it is called, faculty must examine the implicit and explicit assumptions they hold about teaching in order

TABLE 4

Items for Possible Inclusion in a Teaching Portfolio (Part

The Products of Good Teaching

1. Students' scores on teacher-made or standardized tests, possibly before and after a course has been taken as evidence of learning
2. Students' laboratory workbooks and other kinds of workbooks or logs
3. Students' essays, creative work, and project or field-work reports
4. Publications by students on course-related work
5. A record of students who select and succeed in advanced courses of study in the field
6. A record of students who elect another course with the same professor
7. Evidence of effective supervision of honors, master's, or Ph.D. theses
8. Evidence of setting up or running a successful internship program
9. Documentary evidence of the effect of courses on students' career choices
10. Documentary evidence of help given by the professor to students in securing employment
11. Evidence of help given to colleagues to improve teaching

Material from Oneself

This category includes descriptive material on current and recent teaching responsibilities and practices.
12. List of course titles and numbers, unit values or credits, and enrollments with brief elaboration
13. List of course materials prepared for students
14. Information on your availability to students
15. Report on identification of students' difficulties and encouragement of students' participation in courses or programs
16. Description of how films, computers, or other nonprint materials were used in teaching
17. Steps taken to emphasize the interrelatedness and relevance of different kinds of learning

Description of Steps Taken to Evaluate
And Improve One's Teaching

18. Maintenance of a record of the changes resulting from self-evaluation
19. Evidence of having read journals on improving teaching and

attempted to implement acquired ideas
20. Review of new teaching materials for possible application
21. Exchange of course materials with a colleague from another application
22. Research on one's own teaching of the course
23. Involvement in an association or society concerned with the improvement of teaching and learning
24. Attempts to use instructional innovations and evaluate their effectiveness
25. Use of general support services, such as the Educational Resources Information Center, in improving one's teaching
26. Participation in seminars, workshops, and professional meetings intended to improve teaching
27. Participation in course or curriculum development
28. Pursuit of a line of research that contributes directly to teaching
29. Preparation of a textbook or other instructional materials
30. Editing or contributing to a professional journal on teaching one's subject

Information from Others

Students
31. Course and teaching evaluation data that suggest improvements or produce an overall rating of effectiveness or satisfaction
32. Written comments from a student committee to evaluate courses and provide feedback
33. Unstructured (and possibly unsolicited) written evaluations by students, including written comments on exams and letters received after a course has been completed
34. Documented reports of satisfaction with out-of-class contacts
35. Interview data collected from students after completion of a course
36. Honors received from students, such as being elected "teacher of the year"

Colleagues
37. Statements from colleagues who have observed teaching as members of a teaching team or as independent observers of a particular course, or who teach other sections of the same course
38. Written comments from those who teach courses for which a particular course is a prerequisite

TABLE 4 (continued)

39. Evaluation of contributions to course development and improvement
40. Statements from colleagues from other institutions on such matters as how well students have been prepared for graduate studies
41. Honors or recognition, such as a distinguished teacher award or election to a committee on teaching
42. Requests for advice or acknowledgment of advice received by a committee on teaching or similar body

Other Sources
43. Statements about achievements in teaching from administrators at one's own institution or from other institutions
44. Alumni ratings or other graduate feedback
45. Comments from parents of students
46. Reports from employers of students
47. Invitations to teach for outside agencies
48. Invitations to contribute to the literature on teaching
49. Other kinds of invitations based on one's reputation as a teacher (for example, a media interview on a successful teaching innovation)

Source: Shore et al. 1986.

to reflect on what they believe about the teaching and learning process. They will need to deal with some (but certainly not all) of the following assumptions:

- Beliefs about who can and who should benefit from a college education;
- Beliefs about the function of higher education in our society—is it to train or to educate?
- Beliefs about how people learn;
- Beliefs about the best way to teach and whether they can or even want to adjust their teaching style to accommodate diverse learning styles.
- Beliefs about their discipline and its importance to their students' futures.

Everything else that goes into the portfolio should somehow support these beliefs. The primary value of a teaching portfolio derives from the insights faculty gain into their beliefs about how and why others learn. What one believes motivates how he or she acts. If one's belief system is incongruent with her or his behavior, it will be difficult to be an effective teacher. For example, a professor who believes that college should be only for those who have proven themselves capable of learning will likely have great difficulty teaching in a community college whose policy is open-door admissions. Taking time to state their beliefs about teaching and learning forces teachers to make explicit their pedagogical values.

By writing their philosophy of education, faculty will make explicit their values, which will instruct teachers on what *they* believe about how and why students learn. What one believes often influences in subtle ways what one does and says. If faculty believe that students need to be motivated by fear of the dreadful consequences that will accrue from not learning, they are likely to design draconian assignments and tests to induce fear in their students. If they believe that students learn best when gently prodded, they are likely to design their materials quite differently.

Statement of teaching responsibilities

This section of the portfolio simply describes the courses and number of sections taught, enrollment in each, and level of classes (undergraduate lower division, undergraduate upper division, and so on). At multicampus institutions, faculty might want to note the location of the classes.

General goals

A statement of the teacher's general goals for his or her course(s) and how they blend with one's philosophical assumptions might follow the discussion of philosophy. For most, goals will be connected to the specific course, the demands of the discipline, the connection of the course to the overall curriculum, and, one hopes, the needs of students. All of these factors affect how and what a professor teaches. This section might also include some reflection on what faculty members want students to know or be able to do. Faculty might reflect on whether they believe the course content, the discipline's methodology, or critical thinking skills form the essence of what they want students to learn.

A professor's reflections undoubtedly will depend on who is taught and why they are taught. Teaching should be highly situational. Much of what faculty want students to learn will

TABLE 5

Items for Possible Inclusion in a Teaching Portfolio (Part 3)

Roles, Responsibilities, and Goals

- A statement about teaching roles and responsibilities
- A reflective statement about teaching goals and approaches
- A list of courses taught, with enrollments
- A list of clinical teaching assignments, with enrollments
- Number of graduate advisees

Annotated Course Materials

- Syllabi
- Course descriptions with details of content, objectives, methods, and procedures for evaluating students' learning
- Reading lists, assignments, cases
- Descriptions of uses of computers or other technology in teaching
- Nonprint materials and how used

Documentation of Students' Learning

- Graded assessments, including pre- and post-tests
- Students' lab books or other workbooks with written feedback
- Students' papers, essays, or creative works with written feedback
- Publications authored by students
- Records documenting students' work at co-op, intern sites, etc.
- Videotape of student interviews
- Written feedback to teachers from supervisors of clinical, intern, co-op, etc., sites

Evaluations of Teaching

- Summarized student evaluations of teaching, including response rate and students' written comments and overall ratings
- Results of students' exit interviews
- Letters from students, preferably unsolicited

depend on the characteristics of students and their goals. For example, faculty might need to alter their approach (but not their expectations) if they are teaching less-well-prepared students. In some subjects, they might approach teaching majors differently from teaching nonmajors. For example, if a professor's goal is to reduce students' anxiety about studying philosophy, the professor would probably select different readings from those he would select if his goal were to have

- Comments from division head or chair with first-hand knowledge of the individual's teaching
- Letter from colleague who has reviewed the individual's instructional materials

Contributions to Institution or Profession

- Service on teaching committees
- Development of student apprenticeships
- Assistance to colleagues on teaching
- Reviews of forthcoming textbooks
- Scholarly publications in teaching journals
- Work on curriculum revision or development
- Evidence of having obtained funds or equipment for teaching labs, programs
- Provision of training in teaching for students or residents

Activities to Improve Instruction

- Participation in seminars or professional meetings on teaching
- Design of new courses and clerkships
- Use of new methods of teaching, assessing learning, grading
- Research on teaching, learning, assessment
- Preparation of a textbook, courseware, etc.
- Description of instructional improvement projects developed or carried out

Honors or Recognition

- Teaching awards from department, school
- Teaching awards from profession
- Invitations based on teaching reputation to consult, give workshops, or write articles on teaching
- Requests for advice on teaching by committees or other organized groups

Source: Braskamp and Ory 1994.

students understand how Plato and Aristotle shaped the course of Western intellectual history. In other settings, content might be much more important. For example, a faculty member teaching a foundations course in a master's program might need to concentrate on introducing students to basic concepts, theories and authors.

To document and reflect on what, whom, and why they teach, faculty might include several artifacts generated by their teaching. They might include a syllabus, followed by an explanation of how the assignments match whom and why they teach. They might include handouts used in class, with an explanation of how the handouts assist students in achieving goals faculty have for them, or a description of how they assess learning styles and how they accommodate diverse styles (if they do), or annotated examples of students' graded work. But the substance of these sections should be their reflections on how the documents reflect their philosophy of education.

The match between teaching strategies and philosophy

Another section of the portfolio might be usefully devoted to a discussion of how the teaching strategies match one's philosophical assumptions about learning and the goals of the particular course. For example, if teachers believe that students learn best by self-discovery, they might give examples of how class time or out-of-class assignments are designed to lead students to "discover" the intended learning. Or if teachers believe that students learn best when working together, they might show how they incorporate the principles of cooperative learning into their classes. The portfolio's creator might also wish to discuss how the selected teaching strategies match the students' learning strategies.

Documentation of teaching effectiveness and reflection

A portfolio designed to improve teaching needs to include a plan for assessing the success of the faculty member's present strategies. Faculty should also discuss why they believe these techniques accurately assess students' learning. Faculty should include a discussion of the demands of the discipline and those local circumstances that influence decisions about learning outcomes. Assessing effectiveness includes many components. How does one judge whether students learned what one expected they would learn? How does the professor evaluate her or his teaching performance? Assessing teaching and learning requires pedagogical knowledge and skills that many college teachers know little about. In such instances, a portfolio might contain a plan for developing the requisite knowledge (see "Formative Evaluation Techniques" on page 49). Colleges encouraging teachers to complete portfolios, however, may need to commit resources and resourceful teaching specialists to assist faculty in assessing teaching and learning.

The substance of a teaching portfolio, of course, is the documentation of and reflection on the effectiveness of teaching. The content of this section must be determined by the portfolio's owner. A portfolio should use multiple sources and types of data, but it is imperative to understand that no data will substitute for reflection. A portfolio containing only documentation without reflection is simply a receptacle for disposable paper. Moreover, the documentation contained in this section of the portfolio should be selective and representative. A portfolio need not contain everything produced for or by a particular class. Rather, it should contain examples selected because they represent an individual's beliefs about how learning takes place, what strategies are effective in reaching the selected goals, and how the effectiveness of this course, this teacher, and these students are best assessed.

Development of a renewal plan

The portfolio's ultimate value should be the improvement of students' learning. Therefore, the last entry in a portfolio could be a plan for professional development—a plan for how the professor is going to acquire the knowledge, skills, and attitudes that the professor has determined he or she *wants* to gain after reflecting on what has been learned from the process of developing the portfolio. Most portfolios should therefore end with a plan to improve the effectiveness of teaching. For many faculty, doing so might simply involve a few minor adjustments to their method of teaching; for others, it might mean learning more about teaching. Most faculty, however, will need assistance. "Faculty members come to us strong in content and blissfully ignorant of anything having to do with theories of learning and strategies of teaching rooted in pedagogical knowledge of their disciplines. . . . They stand on the shoulders of giants; in their knowledge of teaching, they stand on the ground" (Edgerton 1988, B2). If faculty are to change their teaching styles, some will need assistance from skilled faculty development specialists or master teachers. And it requires that colleges and universities commit resources to the improvement of teaching and learning.

A portfolio might contain a reflective log (Seldin 1991, p. 15). Although finding time to make entries in a reflective log can be difficult for the overworked professor, such a log can unlock the real value of a portfolio. Recording immediate impressions, thoughts on a specific class, disappointments, and thrills, a reflective log can certainly provide its owner copious insights into his or her teaching. Its real value is in the process, not the product. Taking time to record one's thoughts occasions reflection on how one's behavior matches one's beliefs as well as the appropriateness of those beliefs.

Exercises to Get Started

For those having difficulty starting a teaching portfolio, completing the following survey can help. When completing the items, it will help if you not only describe what you do but also explain why you make the choices you do.

1. What is the purpose of your portfolio? Is it for the improvement of teaching, tenure, promotion, or something else?
2. What and whom do you teach? In answering this question, tell what you teach, whom you teach (freshmen, majors, returning adults, for example), whether or not the course is required, how many students are in a typical section, how you would describe the typical student, why they take your course, and so on.
3. Examine the answer to the previous question and describe your purpose in teaching what you select to teach. Is it to prepare students for future course work, employment, or what? Is it remedial? Is it to open students to new experiences and ideas?
4. What teaching techniques or styles do you employ? Why?
5. How do you assess whether students are learning? Why do you assess the way you do? What kinds of assignments, exams, or projects do you use, and why did you select them?

A key component of the teaching portfolio is the statement of your philosophy of teaching. Some prefer to write a "framing statement" of their educational values whose purpose is to put beliefs about the teaching/learning enterprise in perspective and compare what you believe with what you do.

Some teachers find it difficult to write down their educational philosophy. One means of discovering meaning in any aspect of our lives is through metaphor, and many individuals who find it difficult to explain their motives or actions can find a metaphor that sums up what they think. These "guiding metaphors" (Grasha 1990) are intended to explain some major part of our belief system or behavior. Teachers who are trying to state their teaching philosophies can construct a guiding metaphor and thus find the meaning embedded in it.

The following steps are meant to help you get started (see Grasha 1990).

1. Jot down some words and short phrases that describe what you teach, why you teach, how you teach, how you assess students, and so on. The words need not seem connected to one another but should be descriptive and concrete (for example, tough, abstract, traditional, exciting, unexplored). If you are stuck, try looking at the nouns, especially the proper nouns, and jotting down three or four adjectives that come to mind.
2. Scan the words and write down images they suggest. For example, for "complex," one might say "a tangled spider's web," or for "playful," one might say "like a kitten with a ball of string." Some individuals might find it easier to draw a picture or pictures for these first two steps.
3. Look over the words and images you have jotted down for themes. Take the themes you discover and put them into a "guiding metaphor." Try to incorporate as many of the themes as you can into one metaphor that you believe sums up your teaching beliefs and style.
4. Take the metaphor you have devised and elicit what it says about what you believe about teaching.

To illustrate, the words you might have jotted down in the first step could include "discover," "explore," "new," and "uncharted." The images might be explorer, pioneer, astronaut, Lewis and Clark, virgin forest, and wild, untamed rivers. The guiding metaphor might then become an explorer leading a party on a journey to where they have never been, guiding them safely through thick underbrush and overgrown vegetation, and across raging rivers.

Summary

What sets teaching portfolios apart is that they provide instructors with a means to tailor the assessment of teaching and learning to their individual situations. Consequently, the actual content of teaching portfolios will vary from professor to professor. Decisions about what to include depend on the intended use of the portfolio. Therefore, it is important for

When portfolios are to be used to improve teaching and learning, the issue of the assessment's reliability or validity is not paramount.

faculty to know how the portfolio will be used before they start to create one. Teaching portfolios to be used for tenure or promotion should be compiled according to certain standards that specify what the portfolio must contain (student evaluations of faculty, for example), the maximum length, the order of presentation of materials, and so on. Because the standards are meant to ensure that all candidates receive equal consideration, the specific standards are less important than their existence.

Portfolios are collections of documents and artifacts generated in the process of preparing and teaching a course and reflections on how these selected items reveal the quality of one's teaching. Teaching portfolios provide more meaningful data when they are organized in some systematic manner. Moreover, teaching portfolios should be living documents that provide for future changes in one's teaching.

The only essential component of a teaching portfolio is a statement of one's beliefs about teaching, for what one believes about teaching will influence how one teaches. A teacher who believes that his or her students cannot learn will intentionally or unintentionally convey that belief to students. And students will probably meet the teacher's expectations. On the other hand, a teacher who has high expectations and conveys the belief that students can meet them will have "better" students. By devoting the same scholarly methodology and energy to teaching that many professors devote to research, professors can learn how to improve the quality of their instruction.

EVALUATING PORTFOLIOS

If teaching portfolios become part of the documentation used to make summative personnel judgments (tenure, promotion, merit pay, for example), then colleges and universities should decide how they are to be evaluated. In fairness to faculty, the standards should be developed and clearly articulated before anyone begins to develop a teaching portfolio. Two caveats apply to institutions developing criteria to evaluate portfolios. First, the standards will be more effective if they are developed collaboratively by colleagues within a department and explicitly linked to that department's and the college's definition of effective teaching. Second, the criteria should fit the institution's mission. In a community college, for example, if a department's mission is preparing students for transfer, then the criteria should evaluate how well a particular instructor does so. In a graduate school MBA program, if the mission is preparing future business leaders, then the criteria should evaluate how well a particular instructor does so.

Evaluating Qualitative Evidence

In any evaluation system, the type of evidence and the form of assessment differ, depending on purpose. Summative evaluation must, by its very nature, be judgmental; that is, summative evaluation must assign value or worth to the product. On the other hand, formative evaluation should not assign value but should provide specific and detailed analysis of how effectively techniques and strategies were employed to accomplish the desired objectives. Therefore, it is necessary to consider how a teaching portfolio will be used before determining how it is to be evaluated.

When portfolios are to be used to improve teaching and learning, the issue of the assessment's reliability or validity is not paramount. The improvement of teaching and learning *is* paramount, and the very process of developing a teaching portfolio accentuates these issues as much as, if not more than, the assessment of the portfolio. If the teaching portfolio is to be used for summative purposes (such as personnel evaluation), however, it is important that assessment procedures are reliable and valid. Devising reliable and valid techniques for assessment can be somewhat more difficult, because portfolios contain quantitative and qualitative data, and the evaluation of qualitative data can be subjective. "Portfolios do not lend themselves to quick, summary judg-

The improvement of teaching and learning is paramount, and the very process of developing a teaching portfolio accentuates these issues as much as, if not more than, the assessment of the portfolio.

ments about professional accomplishments (such as those achieved by simply counting publications on curriculum vitae). That is, in fact, the primary virtue of portfolios—they reflect the complexity and interrelatedness of all teaching, research, and service activities" (Froh, Gray, and Lambert 1993, p. 109).

Teaching portfolios provide promotion and tenure committees with information about a faculty member's teaching not readily available through other sources (Seagren, Creswell, and Wheeler 1993). But the evaluation of qualitative data also entails certain disadvantages.

> *Most promotion and tenure committees do not have experience in evaluating portfolios; the portfolio requires a greater commitment of time to examine the complete record; and administrators and promotion committees could have more difficulty making qualitative judgments, as teaching history is presented in context rather than in comparison* (Seagren, Creswell, and Wheeler 1993, p. 49).

Although similar concerns are often expressed when campuses discuss teaching portfolios, such concerns are based on the mistaken notion that promotion and tenure committees base their decisions almost entirely on objective, quantitative evidence. The inclusion of qualitative material in decisions about personnel, however, is not new to higher education. Nearly all tenure and promotion committees at any college or university are asked to evaluate the quality of a candidate's teaching, research, and publications. Although administrators are shy to admit it in these litigious times, they are qualitative judgments. Moreover, these judgments are often made without the benefit of explicitly agreed-upon public criteria and hence rely heavily on the subjective beliefs of individual committee members or administrators. The introduction of teaching portfolios does not increase the subjectiveness inherent in evaluation procedures; rather, by adding documentation about the quality of teaching, teaching portfolios add to the completeness of the judgment.

If the purpose of the portfolio is the evaluation of teaching, it will be necessary on many campuses to first dispel the myth that good or effective teaching cannot be defined precisely enough to be evaluated. Faculty often react rather typically.

*Most faculty members did not feel that they could make
qualitative judgments on the dimensions of teaching . . .,
and even those that felt they could did not feel comfortable doing so. They felt that differences were a matter of
"style" or personal preference. Furthermore, some of the
most important objectives of instruction, such as developing thinking skills, fostering multiple viewpoints in students, challenging their stereotypes, or enriching their
appreciation of others, are difficult to readily change
and we do not have adequate measures to show those
changes. Some of these objectives are best justified as
being of value in and of themselves, and difficulty in
relating [them] to demonstrable changes in student learning may subvert attention to them in instruction. At this
point in the development of portfolio review, for accountability purposes it is probably best left up to individuals
who have to make those judgments, such as chairs and
those faculty members serving on promotion and tenure
or awards committees* (Robinson 1993, pp. 16–17).

Although this study was conducted at a single university,
such beliefs are rather pervasive throughout higher education (Massey, Wilger, and Colbeck 1994). Nonetheless, excellent departments that sincerely care about the quality of
teaching will find ways to overcome such complaints. Many
of the efforts to define excellence in teaching are discussed
in "Shaping an Institutional Definition of Good Teaching"
(see page 63). The most effective reply to those who claim
teaching cannot be evaluated is to develop a system and
criteria that work.

Developing Explicit Evaluation Criteria
Developing summative evaluation procedures for teaching
portfolios starts by determining what is to be assessed and
how it will be assessed. The first step is determining what
should be included in the portfolio (see "What Goes into a
Teaching Portfolio?" on page 19). The second step is to define
explicitly the criteria that will be used to evaluate the portfolio. Faculty, particularly departmental faculty, should provide
input for both steps. The content of the portfolio and the evaluative criteria should have some relationship to the demands
of the discipline and the institutional mission. When teaching
portfolios become part of the documentation used to make

summative judgments, it is best to require what must be minimally included (Seldin 1993b). Colleges and universities might also wish to set limits on what can be included, the length of sections, and so on. Requiring common content and setting limits, while potentially somewhat stifling of creativity, provide a common framework for making comparisons among faculty.

When developing holistic criteria for assessing what a teaching portfolio reveals about the quality of teaching, evaluation committees should ask certain key questions.

• Is real evidence of accomplishment presented, not just a reflective statement?
• Is the reflective statement of why and what is done in the classroom consistent with the syllabi and student or peer evaluations of performance?
• Is evidence of students' learning presented, not just material from others and materials from one's self?
• Is an effort to improve performance reflected in the evaluation reports? (Seldin 1992, p. 14).

These questions provide a means to arrive at a general assessment of the portfolio. But evaluators will also need to develop criteria for assessing the specific documents presented in the portfolio. The following five questions could be used for that task.

1. What is the quality of the materials used in teaching?
2. What kinds of intellectual tasks did the teacher set for the students (or did the teacher succeed in getting students to set standards for themselves), and how did the students perform?
3. How knowledgeable is this faculty member in the subjects taught?
4. Has this faculty member assumed responsibilities related to the department's or university's teaching mission?
5. To what extent is this faculty member striving for excellence in teaching? (French-Lazovik 1981, pp. 76–78).

Both set of questions provide starting points for campuses to develop more specific criteria for assessment. Although the criteria work best when tailored to an institution's particular mission, two points must considered. First, active and extensive involvement by faculty in the development of the criteria will be more likely to produce criteria that consider both the demands of the discipline and the institutional mission. Second, those developing the criteria might want to avoid the temptation to overemphasize those aspects of teaching that are easy to quantify. On many campuses, faculty are becoming disheartened over the growing tendency to rely almost exclusively on numerical evidence (such as student evaluations, numbers of publications, amounts of grant monies) for summative types of evaluations.

After explicit criteria have been developed, the next step is to define expected levels of achievement. Evaluation instruments that spell out in as much detail as possible what each achievement level means are preferable. To say that "4" equals excellent performance and "1" equals poor performance for some criterion not only tells the reader very little; it also does not help the professor know how or why it was given. Professors deserve to know, in advance, what it takes to achieve a specific level of performance. If they fail to achieve an adequate or superior rating, they deserve to know specifically what they did not do. For example, if one of the evaluation criteria concerns the quality of the course syllabus, a rating scale might look like this:

1. The instructor provides no syllabus.
2. The instructor provides a syllabus from a previous term that contains inaccurate or outdated material, dates, or references.
3. The instructor provides a syllabus that contains only the information found in the college catalog and/or course schedule.
4. The instructor provides a syllabus that provides a complete course description, course objectives, class meeting times, office hours, basic grading criteria, a tentative schedule of assignments, due dates, and other basic course information.
5. The instructor provides all the above plus detailed explanations of such things as grading criteria, how to study for exams, the objectives of each assignment and class, an explanation of how this course meets the mission of the department and/or the college, and so on.

The exact form each evaluation criterion takes depends heavily on the college's or university's culture and what it values. Therefore, involving faculty in the process of developing the criteria is critical—not only to the acceptance of the criteria, but also to their validity.

Some do not share this preference for explicit criteria, warning of a "crisis in spirit," which can be blamed on the tendency of colleges and universities to move more and more toward explicitly defined evaluation criteria (Whitman and Weiss 1982). While on the one hand using explicit criteria is "fair play," its use might bring out some undesirable faculty behaviors.

> Explicit criteria encourage faculty to do things for the sake of evaluation. A potential abuse is that faculty will meet criteria, but not with the quality or the desired spirit of action. For example, suppose that one criterion of effective teaching is "the instructor provides students with an up-to-date bibliography." A teacher who is intrinsically motivated to conduct the courses may naturally be familiar with new contributions to the literature and will update the bibliography as a matter of course. In this case, we can imagine a teacher who critically reads the literature and thoughtfully adds to and subtracts from the bibliography with [students'] needs in mind. . . . With the advent of explicit criteria, one could now imagine a faculty member adding new citations to the bibliography without having read the new material. . . . In fact, one could even imagine an extrinsically motivated teacher preparing an annotated bibliography based on information provided on book jacket covers and journal article abstracts (Whitman and Weiss 1982, p. 34).

Although the danger exists that a charlatan might attempt to manipulate the system for devious purposes, it is unlikely that a professor could sustain such fakery throughout the entire teaching portfolio. While it might be possible to pass off some inauthentic materials, such as a bibliography based on information provided on book jacket covers and journal article abstracts, most materials would be much more difficult to counterfeit. An instructor who went to all the trouble to develop numerous counterfeit instructional materials to include in a teaching portfolio would have a very difficult time sustaining the effort over an entire course. Moreover, the instructor's colleagues are not fools and would surely recognize the shallowness of such an effort. When a course has no substance, it is highly unlikely that an instructor could create the appearance of substance.

Who Should Evaluate a Portfolio?

Another critical question (when teaching portfolios are evaluated for summative purposes) deals with who should evaluate the portfolio. Several possibilities exist, but when the stakes are high (a decision about tenure, for example), a "campus might well want to cultivate a small group of highly trained portfolio readers, individuals who specialize in particular types of entries or categories rather than being responsible for rating entire portfolios" (Edgerton, Hutchings, and Quinlan 1991, p. 52). While a highly trained group of raters would appear to be desirable, parceling out portions of the portfolio to be separately evaluated could result in a disconnected evaluation report. Effective teaching is a complex act that involves not only several variables, but also the interplay among those variables. Attempting to evaluate teaching in a segmented fashion could obscure those interactions. In fact, "holistic evaluation can be more helpful than a fine-grained, analytic scoring system—a system that was found to turn the evaluation of portfolios into a mechanical task" (p. 52).

The selection of those who are to evaluate the portfolio is integral to the reliability of the results. The selection of evaluators involves some pitfalls:

> . . . too close friendship between [the] candidate and the judges, too few judges, judges lacking sufficient knowledge in the candidate's field, judges in competition with the candidate, lack of anonymity of judges, lack of independence in the judgment process, permitting some peers to act as advocates or adversaries, and failure of peer review committees to provide reasons for negative decisions (French-Lazovik 1981, p. 82).

Yet another consideration concerns the training of evaluators. Most faculty members have little or no formal education in pedagogy or assessment techniques, and most tend to develop their teaching styles by imitation and trial and error. While they might work for developing an individual's teaching style, these techniques seldom provide insights into

The selection of those who are to evaluate the portfolio is integral to the reliability of the results.

other effective teaching styles. Because evaluators of portfolios should be familiar with a variety of teaching styles and approaches for assessing the effectiveness of teaching, some training in the evaluation of teaching and teaching-related documents is necessary. Moreover, in summative evaluations, consistency in judgments is critical. Consistency requires that a single evaluator, judging different portfolios, employs the same criteria and produces similar results (the basis for the reliability of findings) across all portfolios and that different evaluators come to similar conclusions about the same portfolio (the basis for the reliability of evaluators or "interrater reliability"). Training raters can increase the reliability of judgments (Centra 1993), and it can dramatically increase interrater reliability (Root 1987).

Trustworthy Evidence

When the results of the assessment of teaching portfolios are used in personnel decisions, care must be taken to ensure they are used fairly. "The evidence supplied for the assessment of faculty activities and contributions must meet the demands of trustworthiness—dependability, applicability, defensibility, and relevance" (Braskamp and Ory 1994, p. 90). "Four conditions or requirements for trustworthiness . . . are particularly important in faculty assessment: reliability, validity, fairness, [and] social consequences" (p. 91).

Reliability

"Reliability is the degree to which a test consistently measures whatever it measures. The more reliable a test is, the more confidence we can have that the scores obtained from the administration of the test are essentially the same scores that would be obtained if the test were readministered" (Gay 1987, p. 135). Reliability is a necessary, although not sufficient, condition for validity. Two aspects of reliability are to be considered in the assessment of portfolios: "the consistency and dependability of the information" (Braskamp and Ory 1994, p. 91) and the consistency of scores from rater to rater (interrater reliability). Both present special considerations to designers of portfolio projects.

Those interested in ensuring that teaching portfolios provide consistent and dependable information about a professor's teaching can take several steps. Campus leaders interested in improving reliability should pay careful attention to "what documentation is provided to the reviewers, what principles are followed in selecting peer judges, and what procedures govern the conduct of the review process" (French-Lazovik 1981, p. 75). With regard to the documentation supplied the reviewers, campuses should "require portfolios used for tenure and promotion decisions, or teaching excellence awards, to include certain mandated items" (Seldin 1993b, p. 72).

Questions of interrater reliability inevitably arise during the evaluation of qualitative data found in teaching portfolios. The results of one of the few studies of interrater reliability regarding teaching portfolios indicate that when campuses carefully select and train the portfolio evaluators, it is possible to achieve interrater reliability (Centra 1992). That study involved 97 community college faculty members and compared the portfolio ratings of two peers and a dean for reliability. The results from each rater's portfolio evaluation were also compared to results of students' evaluations. The results indicate that thoughtful selection of the raters is a necessary condition for interrater reliability.

In the study, each portfolio was assessed by the appropriate dean, a faculty member selected by the appropriate dean, and a faculty member selected by the faculty member being evaluated. Centra found differences among the raters and that, in general, the ratings given by peers selected by the faculty being evaluated did not correlate with those given by the dean or the faculty member selected by the dean. Moreover, the ratings given by the peers selected by the faculty members being evaluated did not correlate with the student instructional report developed and marketed by Educational Testing Service. But the evaluations of the dean and of the peer selected by the dean did correlate significantly with each other (Centra 1993, p. 11). And the ratings by the dean and by the faculty member selected by the dean correlated significantly with student evaluations.

These findings suggest that if the evaluators are not carefully selected, evaluation of a portfolio by peers may produce varied results, making it difficult to make reliable comparisons among individuals. The selection of the peers by those being evaluated introduces the error(s) resulting in the lack of interrater reliability (Centra 1993). A more random process for selecting raters might increase interrater reliability (French-Lazovik 1981; see also Centra 1993).

Moreover, the absence of interrater reliability in Centra's study was in part the result of the fact that "the peers and deans were largely expected to use their own criteria and standards for judging the portfolios" (p. 14). Training raters of portfolios would likely "make their judgments more valid and reliable" (p. 16), and when evaluators are trained, "a teaching portfolio can be very useful in summative decisions" (p. 16).

When raters were provided some "basic training," "the composite reliabilities of the six raters [were] over 0.900" (Root 1987, p. 79). Moreover, because of the high level of the composite reliabilities, the ratings of three properly trained raters could provide sufficiently reliable judgments for summative evaluation purposes (Root 1987).

Validity

> *The most simplistic definition of validity is that it is the degree to which a test measures what it is supposed to measure. A common misconception is that a test is, or is not, valid. A test is not valid per se; it is valid for a particular purpose and for a particular group. . . . The question is not "valid or invalid" but rather "valid for what or for [whom]"* (Gay 1987, p. 128).

Another way of saying it is that "validity does not refer to the instrument or method of collecting data; rather, it refers to the inferences and generalizations based on the evidence" (Braskamp and Ory 1994, p. 92). Several critical questions regarding the validity of the assessment must first be answered. The primary question is "What are we measuring?" In other words, what are the indicators of good or effective teaching? The next question is "How do local circumstances alter or modify the definition of good or effective teaching?" We know that local circumstances can call for different purposes and outcomes. Another question to address is "What kind of documentation would suffice to indicate good or effective teaching?" Still another key question is "Who is qualified to judge?" "Improved validity depends heavily on what questions are addressed by the review, what documentation is provided to the reviewers, what principles are followed in selecting peer judges, and what procedures govern the conduct of the review process" (French-Lazovik 1981, p. 75).

Fairness

"Fairness" is an imprecise concept that most experts on assessment tend to avoid. Nonetheless, the integrity of any evaluation process depends totally on the fairness of the process and players. Moreover, because reliability and validity are necessary conditions for fairness, some overlap occurs among these concepts. Fairness deals primarily with the adequacy of the evidence; that is, does it reflect the "complexity of the achievements and accomplishments being assessed"? (Braskamp and Ory 1994, p. 92). The adequacy of the evidence can be enhanced by "a strategy called triangulation—gathering, assembling, and combining evidence from a number of perspectives to form an integrated 'picture'" (pp. 82–83). Fairness also involves the adequacy of the judges to make the judgment. That is, fairness requires that the judges have "thorough knowledge of the discipline, . . . what is taught, its accuracy, currency, sophistication, depth, and level of learning it fosters" (French-Lazovik 1981, pp. 74–75).

Social consequences

Social consequences "are the intended and unintended consequences of assessment for the activity and the organization" (Braskamp and Ory 1994, p. 92). Any evaluation process should influence the behavior of those being evaluated. Colleges and universities can design, purposefully or haphazardly, an assessment process that will impact teaching. When professors believe that their performance in the classroom will bring institutional recognition, they will make it a priority. When they believe research and publications will bring institutional recognition, they will make them a priority. Colleges and universities communicate to professors what they should make a priority by the emphasis they place on the activity during the process of evaluation.

The evaluation of teaching portfolios for formative purposes requires a less rigorous methodology than evaluation for summative purposes. Nevertheless, it is still necessary to consider how such an assessment can be used to improve teaching. Even when the aim is to improve teaching, "purposes should drive practice" (Edgerton, Hutchings, and Quinlan 1991, p. 52).

If, for instance, the point is to encourage conversation about teaching across departments that are usually

*isolated from one another, it would make sense to have
an interdisciplinary faculty group-read portfolios. . . . If
. . . the point is to encourage greater attention to the
content-specific nature of teaching . . . , each department might be responsible for reviewing its own portfolios. . . . If the primary thrust of the portfolios is individual improvement, the most powerful context for evaluation might be small groups or pairs of faculty* (Edgerton,
Hutchings, and Quinlan 1991, p. 52).

Summary

The evaluation of portfolios requires careful consideration of
the *purpose* for compiling them. If portfolios are to be used
for summative purposes, special care must be taken to
involve faculty in the development of explicit evaluation
criteria. Moreover, institutions of higher learning must ensure
that the evaluation process and procedures are reliable,
valid, and fair. No one method is best. Rather, the institutional context, the purpose, and the discipline must all be
taken into consideration. "There are no doubt *many* useful
routes to evaluating portfolios" (Edgerton, Hutchings, and
Quinlan 1991, p. 52). The most tragic outcome that could
befall the movement toward using teaching portfolios in
higher education would be to standardize the process and
the evaluation. The appeal of the portfolio, in any profession, comes from its ability to allow the professional to show
his or her individuality and creativity in achieving the mission of the profession.

FORMATIVE EVALUATION TECHNIQUES

Students, oneself, colleagues, and administrators are the primary sources of information that might be used to improve one's teaching. Many institutions have formal processes for gathering opinions and judgments from some or all of these sources—most often in the form of administrative and/or student evaluations. Usually these processes and the data gathered become the basis for making personnel decisions about the individual faculty member. Only rarely do these processes include any formal plan for using the data gathered to improve an individual's teaching. Often this process of gathering information is labeled "summative evaluation."

In addition to summative evaluation, assessment for the improvement of teaching and student learning often includes what many call "formative evaluation." Formative evaluation is intended to provide professors with useful, timely feedback that can be used to improve their teaching and ultimately students' learning. Some commentators on faculty development, hoping to avoid the negative connotations that have sprung up around the concepts of "assessment" and "faculty evaluation," use "informative feedback" rather than formative evaluation (Centra 1993). Despite some disagreement about terms, "among all instructional development efforts the most promising way of fundamentally changing postsecondary teaching is to provide faculty with individualized formative feedback" (Brinko 1993, p. 574).

Whatever it is labeled, if the improvement of teaching and learning is the ultimate goal of a portfolio project, most faculty will need to learn how to assess the effectiveness of their teaching and its effect on students' learning. Although many faculty are quite capable of knowing when students are not getting the material, many do not know how to go about discovering *why* or *what* students are not learning. Incompetence or indifference is not usually the reason for this sad state of affairs. More often, the root cause is that faculty well educated in a discipline lack the knowledge of how to assess their teaching, their students' learning, or their courses. Therefore, the complete portfolio project will plan activities intended to help faculty learn how to assess their teaching, their students' learning, and the currency of their courses.

When we want to know how well we are teaching, we can turn to four primary sources—students, ourselves, colleagues, and administrators. For this discussion, colleagues and administrators are treated as one category. In most situations where

Although many faculty are quite capable of knowing when students are not getting the material, many do not know how to go about discovering why or what students are not learning.

the goal is the improvement of instruction rather than summative evaluation, the administrative assistance comes from the department or division chair. In such cases, it is probably more appropriate to think of the chair as a colleague rather than a supervisor or administrator. The chair should collaborate and facilitate rather than supervise or judge.

Students

Perhaps the best source of information about the effectiveness of one's teaching is students. Students are the only individuals who regularly observe us in action, and it is for their benefit we teach. This symbiotic relationship between professors and students means that it is not only in our best interests to respect what they can tell us about our teaching, but also in their best interests to assist us to improve our teaching.

Techniques for formative evaluation by students range from very formal procedures like Teaching Analysis by Students (TABS) (Clinic to Improve 1974) to more informal classroom research techniques (Angelo and Cross 1993). At the formal end of the spectrum, such techniques look very similar to the student evaluation instruments now widely used in U.S. institutions of higher education (see Seldin 1993a). These evaluations, however, tend to be primarily for summative purposes and frequently carry "sudden-death implications" (Seldin 1993a, p. 6). Because of the serious implications flowing from summative student evaluations, some have suggested that summative and formative evaluation of necessity must be separated, fearing that information that might point to areas needing improvement could become harmful when used in making decisions about personnel.

The issue of whether summative and formative evaluation data can be gathered with the same instrument and/or from the same evaluators often provokes strong conflicting opinions. The modest amount of research available on this issue, however, appears to support those who believe the two functions are compatible (Blackburn and Pitney 1988, p. 17). "Much of the argument on the other side (namely, advocating the split) is theory based. The theoretical argument supporting the split role has to do with role incongruity. How can a supervisor be a helper and a judge at the same time?" (p. 17). It is apparent that the two functions call for different types of questions. Summative evaluations call for a:

*. . . form focusing on global, widely applicable charac-
teristics. . . . But a global rating form of this type is of
limited value for self-improvement purposes, because it
says nothing about idiosyncratic factors in teaching,
fails to specify the reasons for low ratings, and provides
no specific suggestions for improvement* (H. Murray
1987, p. 86).

Several points are to be considered when faculty select or
design formal formative evaluation procedures or instruments. The instrument should be distributed after students
have had sufficient time to observe the teacher's style but at
or before midterm to allow for "midcourse" corrections.
Several studies (see, e.g., McKeachie, Lin, Daugherty, Moffett, Neigler, Nork, Walz, and Baldwin 1980; Overall and
Marsh 1979; Stevens and Aleamoni 1985) have found that
providing faculty with feedback from students at midterm
can improve teaching, especially when the feedback is combined with advice from a faculty development specialist
(Brinko 1993). If faculty conduct evaluations early in the
term, the students who provide the information will gain
some of the benefit from any changes the faculty make.

Unlike summative evaluations, formative evaluation instruments are meant to provide specific, useful feedback to
improve instruction; therefore, formative instruments should
have 20 to 30 items (compared to only a few for summative
evaluation instruments) (Seldin 1989). Some recommend the
use of items that query students about specific teaching
behaviors (H. Murray 1987; Seldin 1989), while others find
open-ended questions more useful (Fuhrmann and Grasha
1983). No researcher seems to have tackled the question of
which is more useful for the improvement of teaching, although in one study faculty preferred items that probe specific teaching behaviors (H. Murray 1987, p. 89). The choice
between items that query students about specific teaching
behaviors or open-ended items would seem to be up to the
preference of the instructor. Most likely, both types of items
would provide useful information to instructors attempting to
improve their effectiveness as teachers. But regardless of the
form the items take, all items should relate to behaviors that
students are in a position to judge reliably. Table 6 provides
some examples of published instruments or procedures avail-

able to faculty for gathering information from students to assess and improve teaching and student learning.

In addition to these more structured approaches, a variety of other creative approaches can be used to gather evaluative data from students. Among them are numerous variations of Small-Group Instructional Diagnosis (SGID), said to have been originally developed at the University of Washington (Braskamp and Ory 1994; Centra 1993). Although the process varies a little from user to user, what is probably the "purest" form of SGID involves the instructor's leaving the class in the charge of an outside facilitator (Coffman 1991). The facilitator asks the students to work in small groups to answer three questions: (1) What do you like about this course? (2) What do you think needs improvement? (3) What specific suggestions do you have for changing this course? (p. 80). Each group must come to a consensus on any point before it can be reported to the whole

TABLE 6

Published Instruments or Procedures for Faculty Evaluati

- H.G. Murray (1987) developed a 60-item diagnostic instrument,* which he did not copyright and encourages others to use. Murray's instrument is valuable because it is well grounded in research—a rarity for formative evaluation instruments. Moreover, this instrument probes specific teaching behaviors —behaviors that, for the most part, the teacher can quickly and easily modify. Although this instrument was designed to gather data from students, it can also be used by colleagues for peer observation.

- Teaching Analysis by Students (TABS) was first developed by researchers at the University of Massachusetts at Amherst (Clinic to Improve 1974) and has been modified and used at many universities and colleges since then. Various forms of the instrument can be found in several different publications (Hilsen and Rutherford 1991; Hoover 1980). TABS probes more general teaching behaviors than H.G. Murray's instrument, and users might therefore find it more difficult to modify behavior without the assistance of a faculty development specialist.

- For those interested in open-ended questions, Fuhrmann and Grasha (1983) provide several forms aimed at probing different aspects of teaching. They offer an open-ended sentence form (p. 197) aimed at getting specific feedback on any aspect of the class. After the groups have developed a consensus, the facilitator asks each group to report its findings to the entire class. The facilitator records the items on the chalkboard. If a majority of the class disagrees with an item, "it is either eliminated or reworded to satisfy the majority of the class members" (p. 81). The facilitator provides the instructor with a written summary and encourages the instructor to discuss the findings with the class. The instructor should tell the class what changes he or she will make and what he or she cannot change and why. SGID has several variations (see J.P. Murray 1991 for a description of a similar technique that an instructor can use without the assistance of a facilitator). Whatever variation is used, faculty could include in a portfolio a summary of a group midterm evaluation, a description of changes made, an evaluation of the effectiveness of the changes, and a reflection on what was learned from the process.

course. They also offer a 59-item student rating form (pp. 201–2) with an interesting twist; they suggest that you ask students to take the three items for which they gave you the lowest score and "list one or two specific behaviors or course incidents that made them give you the rating they did" (p. 200).

- Miller (1987) offers a short (14-item) form for students' appraisal of classroom teaching (pp. 164–65) for faculty interested in getting a quick overview of how their students rate their teaching. Such a form is advantageous because it does not require much class time and can be administered more than once during an academic term.

- Effective teaching requires effective planning; therefore, professors must evaluate not only their teaching, but also their planning. Brinko (1993) offers an 18-item, multiple-choice survey form aimed at assisting professors to design their courses. Once the course has been designed and is being taught, professors might wish to evaluate how well they are accomplishing their goals. Fuhrmann and Grasha (1983) offer a goal assessment form (pp. 198–99) aimed at getting students' opinions on how well the professor is accomplishing goals for the course.

*This instrument and several others can be found in Weimer, Parrett, and Kerns 1988.

Some other creative formats for eliciting students' opinions on how to improve instruction involve techniques that now fall under the rubric of Total Quality Management (TQM) or Continuous Quality Improvement (CQI). Although several variations of TQM in the classroom are available, the most common involve quality circles (Braskamp and Ory 1994; Kogut 1984; Weimer 1990). In business, quality control circles are "committees" empowered to participate in management decisions for the purpose of controlling quality and improving the product. For quality circles to function in a college setting, the professor must sell the concept of a quality circle to the group, instruct the circle in its functions, maintain enthusiasm, and "coach" the group after it begins to operate (Kogut 1984, p. 124). The advantages of quality circles are that students have a vehicle through which they can give "excellent continuous feedback," permitting lectures to be fine-tuned almost daily. Points needing clarification can be reviewed at the next meeting of the class (p. 124). The use of quality circles also has two drawbacks. First, "some sacrifice of course material [is] necessary," which might be more difficult in classes where content is critical. If mastery of content is more critical than exposure to content, however, it might be necessary to sacrifice some content for students to succeed. Second, "quality circles take time and require extra planning" (pp. 124–26).

Many others separately advocated the principal techniques of TQM and CQI long before they became popular on higher education campuses. The use of student committees (see Fuhrmann and Grasha 1983 and McKeachie 1986), for example, is an idea almost identical to the concept of quality circles. A professor would select a committee of three to five students and meet with them regularly. Committee members would solicit the suggestions of other class members (Fuhrmann and Grasha 1983). A variation, called a "senior exit interview," solicits the opinions of seniors after they have completed a course (Braskamp and Ory 1994). Seniors are selected because they may be better able to provide counsel based on a broader perspective.

A faculty member who uses a student committee could ask that committee members periodically provide him or her with summary reports of their findings, which could be incorporated into a portfolio in one of two ways. In some instances, the summaries could provide evidence of quality teaching. In others, the faculty member could explain how his or her teaching changed because of students' comments.

One professor's effort to put into practice the basic tenet of TQM—the belief that customers know what they want—is an attempt to empower her students to make decisions about what they should learn (Rhem 1994). The professor, who structures the assignment carefully, allows students to write the course outline. She consistently finds that students "come up with an outline almost identical to the one she would have written." She also finds that students tend to "give themselves *more* work to do than she would have assigned" (p. 7).

A number of other creative ways can be used to gather opinions from students or to check on how well they are learning what you think you are teaching. One frequently used method involves collecting notebooks from a few students and reviewing them. It is true that what is written in a notebook might not be what the professor said, but if it is written incorrectly (or not at all) in a number of notebooks, it may point to a difficulty with the professor's teaching. Another method is to use e-mail and voice-mail to not only communicate with students but also to assess the effectiveness of one's teaching; classroom faculty could set up a closed conference on e-mail for students to ask questions and make comments about what they are learning and about how teaching might be improved. An e-mail account could be set up in which students can send the instructor anonymous comments about the course (Centra 1993, p. 87). The teaching portfolio could include some of the students' e-mail messages and the professor's reflections on them.

In another innovative technique, students are asked to write a letter to a friend who is considering taking the course (Braskamp, Brandenberg, and Ory 1984). The student should tell the friend about the course and the teaching. The letters should not be signed. Some of these letters or excerpts from them might then be included in a portfolio with the faculty member's reflection on the students' comments. In a course that includes affective goals, a professor might ask students to write letters to him or her describing their changing attitudes (National Center 1993, p. 2).

A program at Brigham Young University pays students to observe a class and consult with the teacher (Sorenson 1994). The student observers, who are invited by the faculty member, receive training that stresses the difference between observation and opinion. After consulting with the faculty, the student observer assumes one of six possible roles:

1. Recorder/Observer: . . . *Student observers record what happened in class . . . focusing on* how *the class proceeded, not necessarily* what *was taught.*
2. "Faux Student": *Here student observers take notes as . . . students enrolled in the class. This role emphasizes recording* what *was taught rather than* how *it is taught.*
3. Filmmaker: *The students film the class and give the videotapes to the instructors.*
4. Interviewer: *The professors leave the class 15 minutes early, and the student . . . [asks students] to write answers to [the following questions]. . . . What should the professor* keep *doing? . . . What should the professor* quit *doing? . . . What should the professor* start *doing?*
5. "Primed Student": *Here the professors tell the student observers what to look for.*
6. Student Consultant: *This model implies an ongoing series of observations and an evolving relationship between the observed and the observers* (Sorenson 1994, pp. 101–2).

Self

Formative evaluations can also include a variety of self-evaluation techniques. The use of these techniques, however, often raises questions about their reliability and validity. When individuals are asked to rate their abilities, they tend to rate themselves higher than colleagues or supervisors would. And it is unlikely that teachers are an exception. In fact, several studies have found low correlations of self-evaluations with those from other sources (Centra 1993). "For instructional improvement, however, self-ratings can be very useful. Studies that compared self- and student ratings indicate that teachers identified the same relative strengths and weaknesses as students did . . ." (p. 97). Moreover, an exhaustive review of the literature points out that "feedback is more effective when information is gathered from oneself as well as from others" (Brinko 1993, p. 577).

Frequently used self-evaluation techniques involve either audio- or videotapes of oneself. Audiotapes allow one to "hear" voice quality, annoying speech tics, and so on. Videotapes allow one to see behavioral tics (such as twirling one's hair, writing on the board with one hand and erasing with the other, and so on). By watching a videotape with the sound turned off, one can analyze "the visual *nonverbal* elements" of one's presentation (Goulden 1991, p. 2). A professor developing a teaching portfolio might include a "before" and "after" tape with reflection about what he or she found on the first tape, what steps he or she took to change teaching behaviors, and how successful the effort was.

Videotaping a class allows instructors to analyze their teaching by applying techniques that usually require a teaching development specialist or a supportive colleague. For example, several of the techniques and instruments mentioned earlier, such as the behavior rating form (H. Murray 1987) or the TABS instrument, could be used by instructors viewing a tape of their teaching. Most authorities strongly recommend the use of a checklist to focus the analysis (see, e.g., Braskamp and Ory 1994, pp. 273–81; B. Davis 1993, pp. 358–60; Miller 1987, pp. 180–81; Weimer, Parrett, and Kerns 1988).

Videotaping a class allows instructors to analyze their teaching by applying techniques that usually require a teaching development specialist or a supportive colleague.

Colleagues

The opinions of colleagues about a professor's research and publication record have long been part of the tenure review process at most universities. Until quite recently, however, few professors would dare consider evaluating a colleague's teaching, much less observe a colleague in the act of teaching. Nonetheless, the trend is growing toward colleagues' helping colleagues improve their teaching. The assistance can take two forms: colleagues reviewing and critiquing the artifacts produced for the course; and colleagues visiting colleagues' classrooms. Few people disagree that a colleague in one's discipline can assist one to improve syllabi, handouts, exams, and so on.

Some skepticism still exists, however, over colleagues' visiting each other's classrooms. Much of the skepticism centers around the notion that colleagues are experts on the subject matter, not on pedagogy, and that reliable agreement among raters is therefore rare. In fact, "research has shown that when colleague ratings of teaching are based solely on classroom observation, only slight interrater agreement can be expected" (Centra 1993, p. 117). But research also demonstrates that "if peer evaluators are given proper training and experience, their ratings based on classroom observations are sufficiently reliable" (Braskamp and Ory 1994, p.

97). Another, potentially more serious, objection concerns the tendency of individuals to favor others who act like they do (p. 98). Greater reliance on evaluation by colleagues could reduce pedagogical diversity within a department or a college—a real danger that requires a thoughtful approach in the creation of a peer review process. Peer observers should be teachers who respect different pedagogical approaches.

Thus, classroom observation by colleagues works best when it is carefully organized. Several conditions are necessary for creating peer observation teams (Miller 1987, pp. 77–78). The observation team should consist of two individuals, one of them from the faculty member's discipline (or a closely related discipline) and the other from a different discipline. Members of peer observer teams should be respected for their teaching ability. The classes to be observed should be selected by the teacher, and three to four visits should occur. Observers should use some sort of checklist (see, e.g., Braskamp and Ory 1994, pp. 270–72; Centra 1993, pp. 209–13; Miller 1987, pp. 166–67; Weimer, Parrett, and Kerns 1988 for examples of checklists).

Based on a review of the literature on observation by colleagues, colleagues can reliably evaluate:

1. *Mastery of course content*
2. *Selection of course content*
3. *Course organization*
4. *Appropriateness of course objectives*
5. *Appropriateness of instructional materials (such as readings, media)*
6. *Appropriateness of evaluative devices (such as exams, written assignments, reports)*
7. *Appropriateness of methodology used to teach specific content areas*
8. *Commitment to teaching and concern for student learning*
9. *Student achievement, based on performance on exams and projects*
10. *Support of departmental instructional efforts* (Cohen and McKeachie 1980, p. 148).

Several models are available for observation by colleagues. A method referred to as "two by two: colleagues as partners in faculty assessment" (Braskamp and Ory 1994, pp.

244–45) involves a minimum of three steps. The first is to get acquainted with the other's teaching goals. Second is an exchange and critique of teaching materials (syllabi, handouts, exams, and so on). And third is a visit to the other's classroom.

A similar collaborative approach also resembles SGID methods (Howe and Moran 1995). Two faculty members collaborate to gather data about students and offer each other advice on how to improve their teaching. After discussing the course objectives, one faculty member visits the other class at midterm.

> *[He or she] asks the students to identify criteria they use to judge the effectiveness of the instructor and course. . . . After the criteria have been agreed upon, the students are asked to discuss how the instructor and course match up with each of these criteria* (Howe and Moran 1995, p. 5).

The colleagues meet and discuss the strengths and weaknesses and brainstorm "ways to improve the course." Then they repeat the process, reversing roles. "The focus of this process is on mutual support. How can we do a better job with our teaching?" (p. 5).

Using another method, graduate students in the M.B.A. program at the University of Chicago can earn one credit by auditing an instructor's class, conducting interviews with focus groups and written surveys of the students, and providing the instructor with weekly reports (Centra 1993). Although not colleagues in the strictest sense, these graduate students are functioning like colleagues while "learning something about teaching" (p. 125).

The Master Faculty program (Katz 1989) pairs colleagues in a highly structured program to improve teaching. Two faculty members are paired; "one of them is the Teacher, the other . . . the Observer. . . . The observer sits in on the class about once a week" (pp. 3–4). Both the teacher and the observer interview two or three students individually weekly. "[They] are not judgmental or evaluative interviews; instead the focus is on how the students go about learning—the students' perceptions of the course content, how they execute their assignments" (p. 4). The colleagues get together once a week to discuss the interviews and the observer's impression of class. At colleges with several colleague pairs, all the pairs get together once a month for a discussion.

Colleagues can also provide valuable assistance without observing a class. Perhaps a colleague could review a few exam papers after they have been graded to check whether the teacher's expectations are too high or too low (McKeachie 1986).

Whatever evaluation techniques are adopted, they should be designed to yield detailed information that can be used by the professor to improve teaching. Formative evaluation works best when "participation is voluntary, nonthreatening, and collaborative—that is, when faculty do not feel the evaluation is being done *to* them" (Kahn 1993, p. 122).

Summary
Although many items can and should go into a teaching portfolio, the heart and soul of a teaching portfolio is the assessment of and reflection on the effectiveness of teaching and learning. Most faculty members will need some assistance in designing processes for evaluating their teaching. Such assistance can come from the chair of the department or a faculty development specialist, but the primary sources of knowledge about the effectiveness of one's teaching are students, oneself, colleagues, and administrators.

Gathering data on one's teaching demonstrates a concern for the quality of teaching. A variety of published and easy-to-use instruments are available for gathering data from any or all of these sources. Several creative and nontraditional means of gathering data are also available, some of which are adaptations of TQM or CQI techniques. It is probably true that the method of gathering data is less important than the act of gathering them.

In addition to input from students, faculty can ask colleagues to assess the quality of their teaching, and colleagues can provide some valuable insights about materials designed by instructors. It is important to remember, however, that if faculty are going to visit each other's classrooms, some form of structure is needed. Faculty can also evaluate themselves, although self-evaluations are less reliable than other forms of evaluation.

SHAPING AN INSTITUTIONAL DEFINITION OF GOOD TEACHING

Before colleges and universities can implement teaching portfolios, they need to grapple with the task of defining good teaching. If colleges and universities intend to include standards for good teaching when making personnel decisions, they need to be able to recognize good teaching. Moreover, if colleges and universities intend to use portfolios to assist professors in their efforts for continuous improvement of teaching, administrators and professors need to be able to recognize good teaching. Professors creating portfolios and using some of the assessment techniques described in the previous section need some standards for interpreting the data. In other words, before we can measure something, we need to locate or create a properly calibrated yardstick.

Despite the importance publicly placed on teaching, most colleges and universities have neglected to define good teaching. Professors traditionally have enjoyed great freedom from the kind of curriculum and classroom control often found in grades K–12. Consequently, professors usually treat teaching like a private affair that goes on behind closed doors. Many administrators worry that if they intrude too much in this private sphere, they will not only anger professors, but also bring accusations of violating academic freedom. Hence, administrators tend to rely on rather vague definitions of teaching for fear of treading on academic freedom.

Professors and administrators often argue that "good" teaching cannot be defined or that a single definition would be woefully inadequate. It is said that teaching is an ineffable quality that one either has or does not have, and no one can be taught to teach. Research findings in cognitive psychology, learning styles, and teaching styles are proving these statements to be myths, however. This section demonstrates that good teaching *can* be described and that *many* reasonable definitions exist. The definition of good teaching depends on the purpose, and definitions will vary if the purpose varies. Although some of the literature reviewed in this section contradicts other cited studies, each could be valid in different settings.

Colleges can begin to develop a communal definition of good teaching by encouraging teachers to engage in conversations about teaching. Many observers (e.g., Astin 1993; J. Davis 1994; Edgerton 1993; Palmer 1993; Shulman 1993) have argued that teaching will never achieve the status it deserves until it becomes "community property" (Shulman

1993) or until we create "good talk about good teaching" (Palmer 1993).

Teaching occurs in remarkable isolation of one's colleagues. Professors often enter the classroom, close the door, and teach without benefit of peer opinions. While professors do not hesitate to seek colleagues' advice about research, they rarely seek advice about teaching. "By privatizing teaching we make it next to impossible for the academy to become more adept at its teaching mission. The growth of any skill depends heavily on honest dialogue among those who are doing it" (Palmer 1993, p. 8). The result is that professors "will perform the function conservatively, refusing to stray far from the silent consensus on what 'works'—even when it clearly does not" (p. 8).

Although a public dialogue on teaching may not produce a definitive definition of good or effective teaching, it can enrich and deepen our understanding of teaching in all its various guises. Such a dialogue, however, must be grounded in the differences created by discipline (Cross 1993; Shulman 1993), type of student, and institutional mission (Kahn 1993; Seldin 1992).

Any definition of effective teaching needs to be closely connected to the goals of a particular course and the objectives of the specific curriculum containing the course. The curricula and course goals should be influenced by the type of institution and academic department that offers the course. A philosophy department at a research institution offering a course in ancient philosophy to doctoral candidates will (or should) have quite different goals [from] a community college offering ancient philosophy to satisfy a general education degree requirement for allied health majors (J.P. Murray 1995b, p. 167).

Any attempt, therefore, to define good or even effective teaching must take into account that "instructional methods and content are discipline-specific, making absolute comparisons both impossible and inappropriate" (O'Neil and Wright 1992, p. 6).

Because much of the discussion of how to improve teaching focuses exclusively on technique, it often seems to be shallow and hollow. Although the hollowness emanates from several sources, the primary source appears to be the tendency of some to divorce the dialogue about teaching from a dialogue about learning. "If deepening the dialogue about teaching is the goal, this deeper conversation will occur when we talk with faculty in increasingly sophisticated ways about learning, when we help them distinguish among different kinds of learning, and [when we] encourage them to select teaching strategies based on learning" (J. Davis 1994, pp. 44–45).

Colleges and universities have concentrated on the improvement of teaching for a long time, assuming that if teachers perfected their techniques, students would automatically learn—all of which leads to the view that if we can make professors better teachers, students will learn. This tendency creates a sterile view of teaching that often makes no effort to assess how, what, or whether students learn. "Student outcomes under the current paradigm are irrelevant to the successful functioning of a college" (Barr 1995, p. 2). Moreover, faculty development:

> . . . [often] focuses on the improvement of teaching and often occurs in splendid isolation from the important issues of curriculum content and assessment of student learning outcomes. What appears to be developing are three separate literatures, three sets of professional associations (or subsidiary efforts within associations) [that] deal separately and sometimes exclusively with curriculum planning, improving teaching, and assessment. Much of this activity and the emerging literature is quite valuable, but [it] is compartmentalized and specialized (J. Davis 1994, p. 45).

The Current State of Knowledge about Good or Effective Teaching

Three types of literature are generally available regarding good teaching—statements of personal convictions based on years of observations and study (e.g., Eble 1988, Lowman 1984), statistical or quantitative studies that seek the opinions of faculty and/or students, and ethnographic or qualitative studies. Taken together, they might provide us with a comprehensive view of "good teaching"; however, each type of literature has drawbacks. Statements of personal convictions represent primarily the opinions of the authors and cannot be generalized without risk. Quantitative studies seek the opinions of college teachers and students and often are not validated against any criterion of learning. Moreover, quantitative studies use statistical techniques to analyze the data for commonalities that may overlook important individual differences (i.e., "outliers") in teaching and learning. Qualitative studies are also based on the collective opinions of the subjects and also are not generalizable.

Statements of personal convictions

Based on their research, Chickering and Gamson (1987) provide one of the most influential statements of personal convictions. According to them, in teaching:

1. *Good practice encourages student-faculty contact.*
2. *Good practice encourages cooperation among students.*
3. *Good practice encourages active learning.*
4. *Good practice gives prompt feedback.*
5. *Good practice emphasizes time on task.*
6. *Good practice communicates high expectations.*
7. *Good practice respects diverse talents and ways of learning* (Chickering and Gamson 1987, p. 1).

Statistical or quantitative studies

Like most statements of personal convictions, Chickering and Gamson's list emphasizes the quality of teacher-student interaction. A reader will search this list in vain for any mention of "knowledge of subject matter," which nearly all quantitative studies of good or excellent teaching consider to be a major criterion. Statistical studies more often point to teachers', rather than students', behaviors or characteristics.

One study using a Delphi technique, for example, found that faculty development leaders in "nationally known teaching initiatives at a variety of institutions" believed good teaching required the 27 competencies listed in table 7 (Smith and Simpson 1995). Meta-analysis of more than 70 studies (Feldman 1976) found that, from students' point of view, effective teachers demonstrate knowledge of subject matter, love of the discipline, and love of teaching. Students also say that effective teachers are organized, clear, and prepared. And another review of the literature found that students consistently identified eight characteristics in effective teachers.

1. Knowledge of the subject matter.
2. Interest in, concern for, and respect for students.
3. Well prepared/well organized.
4. Enthusiasm about/interest in the subject matter, dynamic, energetic, stimulates interest.
5. Ability to present material interestingly and clearly.
6. Openness, respect for opinions of others, encouragement of questions and discussion.
7. Fairness.
8. Helpfulness and availability (Bernoff 1992).

Studies of excellence in teaching at community colleges paint a similar picture. Faculty and administrators at Miami-Dade Community College produced the list of "core characteristics" in table 8 that define excellent teachers.

Several interesting observations can be made about these lists. First, all the lists contain only behaviors, attitudes, and qualities that relate to *teachers*. None speak to the behaviors, attitudes, and qualities of students that might enhance their learning. Several researchers and theorists, however, are now arguing that students have some (not all) responsibility for the quality of their learning experiences (see, e.g., Gardiner 1994). Second, only the Miami-Dade Community College study includes any intended outcomes for student behaviors or attitudes. Although these research findings are undoubtedly important, they tend to view the teaching-learning equation from only one side.

Ethnographic or qualitative studies
Qualitative studies of excellent college professors most often emphasize the effects on and interaction with students. For example, an in-depth qualitative study of five excellent community college teachers found that all five exhibited:

1. A strong command and organization of their subject;
2. Enthusiasm about their discipline and class presentations;
3. An approachable and friendly style with students; and
4. The ability to motivate students to form goals and succeed academically (DuBois 1993, p. 468).

TABLE 7

Competencies Required for Good Teachers

1. Provide helpful feedback to students in a variety of ways.
2. Exhibit respect and understanding for all students.
3. Demonstrate mastery of the subject.
4. Communicate effectively in both written and oral formats in English.
5. Develop a reflective approach to teaching by collecting feedback and using it to continually modify the approach to teaching.
6. Promote students' individual involvement through learner-centered teaching methods.
7. Enhance students' motivation through personal enthusiasm for the subject.
8. Communicate and manage appropriate expectations for achievement in the course.
9. Demonstrate a general belief that all students are capable of learning.
10. Encourage cooperation and collaboration among students.
11. Select course material suited to students' backgrounds, abilities, and interests.
12. Construct valid and reliable tests and administer other evaluation measures fairly.
13. Be accessible to students.
14. Match varying teaching methods with specific instructional objectives.
15. Accommodate students' different learning styles by using a variety of teaching methods.

Excellent community college faculty also:

1. Spent a considerable amount of time preparing course presentations;
2. Were talented in clarifying difficult subject matter;
3. Were accessible to students outside class;
4. Evaluated their students frequently and always let them know where they stood with regard to academic performance;
5. Had a strong sense of commitment and dedication to community college teaching;
6. Understood that many community college students come from troubled family experiences and lack academic skills;
7. Were able to convey a strong sense of presence in the

16. Present material that is sequenced and paced appropriately for learners.
17. Recognize and accept teaching as a fundamental and challenging dimension of scholarship.
18. Enhance students' motivation by demonstrating the subject's relevance to their future needs and goals.
19. Manage the learning environment so that maximum learning will result.
20. Lead class discussions that stimulate learning and enhance the goals of the course.
21. Manage the process of planning, teaching, and evaluating in a timely manner.
22. Communicate important values inherent to the discipline or profession.
23. Use research in teaching as it applies to instruction in one's field.
24. Build confidence in students by helping them to successfully meet learning objectives.
25. Deal appropriately with issues that relate to various aspects of diversity.
26. Design courses that challenge students to pursue higher-level learning.
27. Deal appropriately with matters of discipline, academic honesty, and legal information.

Source: Smith and Simpson 1995, p. 228.

classroom to elicit students' attention and stimulate their emotions;
8. Never embarrassed or berated students;
9. Encouraged students' participation; and
10. Saw themselves as student-centered teachers (DuBois 1993, p. 464).

Such teachers clearly are committed to students.

These results are similar to those of others who have studied excellent community college instructors. For example, a study of 289 instructors at community colleges in the Midwest concluded that "the most important quality or characteristic of successful community college instructors is a genuine interest in working with a diverse student clientele. Success in teaching appears to be focused as much on the

TABLE 8

Core Characteristics for Excellent Teachers

A. *Motivation.* Excellent faculty members at Miami-Dade Community College, whether classroom teachers, librarians, counselors, or serving in any other faculty capacity:
1. Are enthusiastic about their work.
2. Set challenging individual and collective performance goals for themselves.
3. Set challenging performance goals for students.
4. Are committed to education as a profession.
5. Project a positive attitude about students' ability to learn.
6. Display behavior consistent with professional ethics.
7. Regard students as individuals operating in a broader perspective beyond the classroom.

B. *Interpersonal Skills.* Excellent faculty members at Miami-Dade Community College, whether classroom teachers, librarians, counselors, or serving in any other capacity:
1. Treat all individuals with respect.
2. Respect diverse talents.
3. Work collaboratively with colleagues.
4. Are available to students.
5. Listen attentively to what students say.
6. Are responsive to students' needs.
7. Are fair in their evaluations of students' progress.
8. Present ideas clearly.
9. Create a climate that is conducive to learning.

interaction with students as on the transmission of content" (Higgins, Hawthorne, Cape, and Bell 1993, p. 34).

Effective community college teachers also have certain "hidden characteristics."

1. They overcame childhood hardships and became attracted to the helping professions;
2. They were inspired by past teachers;
3. They have a distinct identity as a teacher/messiah; and
4. They need students as much as, if not more than, their students need them (DuBois 1993, p. 465).

It is doubtful that these characteristics are necessary to be an effective community college teacher, but they might provide some insight into how and why some individuals become effective community college professors.

C. *Knowledge Base*. Excellent faculty members at Miami-Dade Community College, whether classroom teachers, librarians, counselors, or serving in any other capacity:
1. Are knowledgeable about their work areas and disciplines.
2. Are knowledgeable about how students learn.
3. Integrate current subject matter into their work.
4. Provide perspectives that include a respect for diverse views.
5. Do their work in a well-prepared and well-organized manner.

D. *Application of Knowledge Base*. Excellent faculty members at Miami-Dade Community College, whether classroom teachers, librarians, counselors, or serving in any other capacity:
1. Provide students with alternative ways of learning.
2. Stimulate intellectual curiosity.
3. Encourage independent thinking.
4. Encourage students to be analytical listeners.
5. Provide cooperative learning opportunities for students.
6. Give constructive feedback promptly to students.
7. Give consideration to feedback from students and others.
8. Provide clear and substantial evidence that students have learned.

Source: McCabe and Jenrette 1990, pp. 189–90.

Some new faculty members become good teachers and others do not. Interviews of four cohorts of new faculty at two universities over a five-year period (1985–90) identified the seven characteristics that led a few to be successful teachers (although the findings paint a bleak picture for anyone aspiring to enter the professorial ranks) (Boice 1991).

1. Positive attitudes about students;
2. Lectures paced in relaxed style so as to provide opportunities for students' comprehension and involvement;
3. Low levels of complaining about their campus, including collegial supports;
4. Evidence of actively seeking advice about teaching often from a colleague;
5. A quicker transition to moderate levels of preparing lectures;

6. A generally superior investment in time spent on scholarly and grant writing (a mean of 3.3 hours per work week);

7. A great readiness to become involved in campus faculty development programs.

Summary

A necessary first step toward effectively evaluating and developing good or excellent teaching is to define excellence in teaching. Any definition of teaching, however, must take into account differences in disciplines and institutions. Moreover, definitions of effective or excellent teaching will be impoverished if they fail to include a dialogue about what it means to be an effective learner.

The literature abounds with definitions of effective teaching, and all are somewhat different. All of these writers and researchers, however, seem to have concluded that excellent teachers are ones who care about the *learner* as well as the *learning process*. This caring appears in the form of understanding that learners are individuals with individual differences. Moreover, excellent teachers believe that their students *can* achieve and communicate this belief in a number of ways, including setting high standards. Another striking feature of all these definitions is that they emphasize that learning and teaching are more effective when done collaboratively. Perhaps most important, all conclude that the improvement of teaching and learning is possible and that teachers—through their behaviors and attitudes—can make a difference.

THE ORGANIZATIONAL CULTURE AND TEACHING PORTFOLIOS

Organizational theorists have long recognized that universities and colleges develop their own cultures and socialize new members into that culture in a variety of ways (Tierney and Rhoads 1993). Consequently, change agents need to respect the existing culture while at the same time attempting to alter it (Fife 1993). Nonetheless, change agents must make deliberate, well-thought-out attempts to change the culture. "A definition of insanity is to do the same thing the same way but expect different results. If institutions wish to change their outcomes, they must be willing to examine the interrelated activities that make up the system that produces the outcomes" (Fife 1993, p. xiv). This section explores the existing culture of higher education and how administrators and faculty might go about altering that culture to introduce the concept and practice of teaching portfolios.

Concern is growing that "faculty-bashing is becoming a growth-industry."

Evaluating the Current Reward System

Concern is growing that "faculty-bashing is becoming a growth-industry" (Edgerton 1993, p. 22), and one observer, only slightly tongue in cheek, suggests that "such denunciations seem well on the way to becoming the cliche opening for articles describing the state of higher education in our time" (J.P. Murray 1995b, p. 163). When higher education occasionally came under attack in the past, college and university administrators typically dismissed such criticism as coming from the uninformed rabble, who, because of their lack of education (perhaps also their lack of the ability to benefit from a higher education), could not understand the lofty mission of higher education.

Administrators may want to respond proactively this time around. While it is impossible to say that the criticisms will not fade away, the mood of the public and their legislators is quite different this time. The public has come to see higher education as a right, not a privilege. The rapidly rising costs of college, coupled with the perceived decline in accessibility for the children of the middle class, generate considerable hostility and demands for public accountability. Moreover, the public no longer assumes that higher education's leaders are morally and/or intellectually superior to other institutional leaders. Publicity about scandals involving the misuse of public funds contributes to the feeling that colleges and universities are populated with humans no less corruptible and no less fallible than those who populate other social institutions.

Elected officials have responded eagerly to the public's misgivings by introducing legislation to regulate colleges and universities. In 1994, Committee C of the AAUP reported that "eight states currently have some type of legislation [to increase the hours professors spend in the classroom] and it is under serious consideration in six others" (American Association 1994, p. 3). As of 1995, Connecticut, Ohio, Maryland (which also withheld $21.5 million until universities could prove they had increased faculty workload), Massachusetts, and Washington had all passed legislation intended to increase the teaching loads of college faculty, and Colorado, Georgia, Minnesota, New York, Oregon, and Wisconsin were seriously considering similar legislation (Cage 1995, p. A33). Such legislation, while misguided, should send a strong signal to higher education.

Even within the academy, a growing number of voices advocate change. If we are to take them at their word, the American professoriat believes that colleges and universities must undergo a radical realignment of priorities (Braskamp and Ory 1994; Edgerton 1993). Several studies have shown that professors believe that their institutions do not recognize good teaching, despite the fact that most professors report that teaching well is an important personal priority. In one study of 35,000 professors, 98 percent responded that being a good teacher was very important to them; nonetheless, only 10 percent believed their colleges or universities rewarded good teaching (Higher Education 1991). A survey of 900 full-time faculty teaching in the University of California system found that only 7 percent believed the system rewarded good teaching (Edgerton 1993, p. 13).

Professors have become quite vocal about their belief that research brings rewards and good teaching does not. In an article reporting on a forum on faculty roles and rewards, one professor was quoted as saying, "I feel pressured to do research in order to get rewards for myself, at the expense of my graduate students" ("Thoughts from" 1993, p. 18). Lesley Stahl, in a recent segment on *60 Minutes,* lambasted the research culture that pervades higher education. When she asked a University of Arizona professor what it took to gain tenure, he replied, "write and write, and publish and publish, and get grants and get grants." After the University of Arizona's provost talked with the professor in an attempt to reconcile his disgruntled beliefs with those of the university's administrators, he remained adamant that publishing was the determinant of promotion. The professor told a *Chronicle of Higher Education* reporter, "When it comes down to an appeal from an associate professor who has done what I've done with undergraduate education, they turn a deaf ear. . . . The message is very clear: Teaching doesn't count" ("In Box" 1995, p. A16). The chair of the Commission of Inquiry on Canadian University Education, Stuart Smith, put it this way: "It is now politically correct to speak favorably of teaching. . . . But a researcher who can barely express an idea outside the laboratory can still make it to the top" (Fennell 1992, p. 57).

Some inconsistencies are apparent between what professors do and what they say, however. Despite the finding that 98 percent of faculty claim teaching is very important to them, "just 58 percent of faculty in four-year schools say their chief interest lies in the classroom; since 1969, the percent of faculty agreeing that teaching should be the primary criterion for promotion fell from 78 percent to 62 percent" (Meacham 1993, p. 42). In other words, it may not be only administrators, alumni, trustees, and donors who covet the prestige of being connected to a prominently recognized research university. But despite the apparent contradictions between professors who say they value teaching more than research and those whose actions say they value research, it is clear that faculty are right when they claim that their institutions value research. Clearly, the rewards go to the researchers.

Rewards for Research

Researchers found that at four-year colleges and universities, the amount of time spent teaching or in contact with students was inversely proportional to salary. "Overall, faculty are paid a low of $34,307 if they spend more than 72 percent of their time teaching and a high of $56,181 for spending less than 35 percent of their time teaching" (National Center 1993, p. 1). In contrast, "salaries range from a high of $50,060 for those spending more than 34 percent of their time on research to a low of $30,389 for those spending less than 5 percent of their time on research" (p. 2).

The 1987–88 National Survey of Postsecondary Faculty (4,481 faculty) found that teaching is woefully unrewarded and consequently neglected at four-year colleges and universities (Fairweather 1993). The reason for the neglect of teaching in favor of research is quite clear. "The more time faculty spend on teaching, including hours in the classroom, the lower the pay" (p. 46). The exceptions are said to be four-year undergraduate liberal arts colleges and community colleges. A close examination of the tables in the report, however, reveals that even this statement is misleading. Although those who spend more time teaching at liberal arts institutions do receive slightly better pay than colleagues at the same institution who spend less time teaching, they on the average are still compensated at a lower level than their colleagues at research institutions. Moreover, even at liberal arts institutions, where research and publication ostensibly are less emphasized, "the more time spent on research and the greater the scholarly productivity . . . the greater the pay" (p. 46). Community colleges are not included in these data and, because they publicly pronounce themselves dedicated to teaching over research, may be an exception. The lack of emphasis on research at community colleges, however, does not automatically mean that teaching is emphasized. The few studies available on community colleges, for example, suggest that good teaching is not consistently rewarded (J.P. Murray 1995a).

Despite the growing criticism, enthusiastic defenders of the research culture still exist. Peter Frost, associate dean of the Faculty of Commerce and Business Administration at the University of British Columbia, maintains that "the bias is towards research because it is the research that keeps things moving forward" (quoted in Fennell 1992, p. 58). "Keeping things going" means many things to administrators. For most, it means attracting financial support in the form of large grants and gifts. The financial support, according to the defenders of the research culture, is what attracts graduate students (Fennell 1992). Moreover, in response to Lesley Stahl's story on *60 Minutes,* University of Arizona President Manuel T. Pacheco circulated an e-mail answer that argued that research dollars pay for "80 percent of the equipment used by our undergraduates in science" and "have constructed buildings, outfitted laboratories, and supported thousands of [students] with on-campus jobs that give them real-world experience in their career field."

Some argue that research keeps universities not only financially healthy, but also intellectually healthy. William Leggett, academic vice president at Montreal's McGill University, says that "unless a professor is at the forefront of his discipline, he will be reduced to lecturing from a textbook. . . . The best teachers appear capable of balancing both functions" (Fennell 1992, p. 58). Despite such claims, researchers have not been able to find a positive correlation between being a good teacher and being a productive researcher. Even if a correlation exists between effective teaching and productive research, it is unlikely to affect undergraduate education. In fact, the average correlation in one study was about .13 (Feldman 1987). Moreover, at most universities, researchers are released from classroom responsibilities if they secure sufficient grant funding. "Recent studies by universities in several states found that, on average, full-time faculty taught less than one-quarter of all undergraduate courses. . . . Research cannot enhance undergraduate teaching when the full-time faculty doing research are not teaching undergraduate students" (Fairweather 1993, p. 44).

Even when campuses attempt to reward good teaching, they sometimes do things that hurt more than help. For example, the University of North Carolina at Chapel Hill awards a three-year distinguished teaching award that pays an annual bonus of $5,000. At the end of the three years, however, the money goes away (Meacham 1993, p. 44). In other words, being excellent at teaching can lead to a temporary salary increase and a drastic salary reduction when the award expires. In most cases, professors who win salary increases for productivity in research do not lose the increase even if their productivity falls off.

Despite the tendency to put the conflict between research and teaching in extreme terms, the resolution may not require a radical restructuring of colleges and universities. The real conflict appears to be balancing the need for both and rewarding teaching equally with research. Balancing the two starts with the recognition that both are time-consuming. Effective teaching takes time away from research, and, with the average professor's work week now estimated at 54 hours (Edgerton 1993, p. 13), the time to teach well must come from the time a professor devotes to research or to family. Colleges and universities must find ways to balance the conflicting claims research and teaching make on a professor's time. Moreover, and most important, administrators must find ways to demonstrate that they value good teaching no less than they value good research.

Colleges and universities must find ways to balance the conflicting claims research and teaching make on a professor's time.

Changing the Reward Structure to Emphasize Teaching

The pivotal first step requires institutions to examine critically what they value, for what institutions value is ultimately reflected in their reward structure. On the whole, four-year colleges and universities reward research, and until this situation changes, in action as well as in word, teaching will always take a distant second place to publications, grants, and the other public marks of the researcher. It "is futile to talk about improving the quality of teaching if, in the end, faculty are not given recognition for the time they spend with students" (Boyer 1990, p. xi). A critical first step to recognizing and rewarding good teaching is to develop effective ways to assess teaching performance. The primary argument of this monograph is that *teaching portfolios provide a superior means of assessing teaching and improving learning.*

Appraisal of teachers' performance must be individualized for it to ultimately affect teaching (Blackburn and Pitney 1988). "Individualization in teaching is threatened by the typical way it is assessed, namely, by student evaluations. . . . They establish a uniform set of standards and assume that certain behaviors are good, and the absence of those behaviors constitutes proof of poor teaching" (p. 32). Even if the uniform set of standards are valid, student evaluations alone appear to have little impact on the improvement of teaching (Ory 1991). Therefore, something more is needed if colleges and universities seriously desire to improve teaching through appraisal of performance. "A portfolio system would accomplish the goal of continuous growth and development, the realization of the individual's full potential" (Blackburn and Pitney 1988, p. 32).

The individualization of the evaluation of teaching provides the power and promise to the portfolio movement. Portfolios allow individuals to document what they do, how well they do it, and, most important, *why* they do it. In other words, portfolios provide instructors with a means to "express in their own way the unique aspects of their teaching and the variety of reliable data [that] demonstrate it" (Fayne 1991, p. 5). Thus, "portfolios enable teachers to document their teaching in an authentic setting and to bring in the context of their own classrooms. . . . And when the actual artifacts of teaching are combined with a teacher's reflections, portfolios permit us to look beneath the surface of the performance itself and examine the decisions that shaped a teacher's actions" (Wolf 1991, p. 136).

Portfolios provide an authentic assessment that connects context to outcomes in a concrete, individualized manner befitting a professional. Portfolios empower a professional to take charge of his or her professional life and critically reflect on it with an eye toward improvement. "The process forces them to (1) think about their teaching activities; (2) assess priorities; (3) ponder teaching strategies; and (4) plan for the future. . . . The teaching portfolio is an effective tool for instructional improvement because it is grounded in discipline-related pedagogy" (Seldin 1992, p. 14).

Among the advantages that teaching portfolios bring to higher education, two are of importance to those wishing to alter the culture of higher education. First, portfolios can be powerful instruments for the improvement of teaching; that is, they can combine evaluation and faculty development. Second, teaching portfolios provide a means to publicly showcase and reward effective teaching while acknowledging differences in disciplines. Although certain common pedagogical principles cut across the disciplines, certain clear differences are grounded in the disciplines. "Teaching goals in the disciplines are visibly and legitimately different. . . . If teachers from different disciplines have different teaching goals, then a variety of measures must be used to assess teaching effectiveness" (Cross 1993, p. 220). Obviously, student rating forms that reduce assessment of the effectiveness of teaching to a set of behaviors common to all disciplines cannot account for the differences among disciplines. Teaching portfolios can, because they force teachers to ask themselves about what they teach and why they teach it. Only others from one's discipline can assist in answering these questions.

Although examining and changing the reward structure is a necessary first step for any college or university desiring to emphasize the importance of teaching, it is not sufficient to unseat the dominant culture of "the researcher." Nor is it likely to sell the concept of teaching portfolios to a cynical faculty that believes teaching does not count for much. Recently, the dean of the School of Education at a Research I University said, "Teaching can't get you tenure, but bad teaching can get you fired." Another Research I University proudly announces in its catalog that it honors authors of one or more books with membership in a special faculty club and that those who publish a substantial number of articles in peer-reviewed journals also have their own faculty club. Being intelligent folk, faculty obviously get the message when they cannot find a club for honored teachers with mediocre publishing records. The sad part is that such activities are so ingrained into faculty members' thinking that they are rarely offended by the clear emphasis on research over teaching.

Introducing the concept of teaching portfolios at such universities is likely to be greeted with the same enthusiasm a screen door salesman receives on a submarine. Although both examples in the previous paragraph came from research universities, the climate is not likely to be any warmer on four-year liberal arts or community college campuses. Many four-year liberal arts colleges aspire for equality with their university counterparts and believe placing more emphasis on research and publications will achieve this goal—witness the number of undergraduate liberal arts institutions that have recently dropped the word "college" from their name in favor of "university." Moreover, even at undergraduate liberal arts institutions, those with better publication records receive higher pay (Fairweather 1993). Community colleges may not emphasize research and publication, but their faculty frequently tend to react negatively to any change in the way they are evaluated.

Other Changes Needed

Understanding the culture of the organization and how change can be effectively introduced is necessary if the concept of teaching portfolios is to be successfully introduced. Several aspects of an academic institution's culture must be respected if the change agent is to be successful, and several aspects are critical if teaching portfolios are to be successfully introduced on campus.

First, faculty must be convinced that the idea is a good one and will benefit them (Kremer, Malik, and Hazer 1993; Seldin and Annis 1990). Faculty are often deeply suspicious of any new evaluation technique (J.P. Murray 1994b) and must be assured that it will not be used against them. Administrators should be very candid about the purpose and anticipated outcomes of any evaluation technique (Blackburn and Pitney 1988), and faculty should be involved in deciding "the criteria to be used, . . . the evidence by which performance will be appraised, and . . . the manner in which the evaluation will be conducted" (p. 38). Moreover, faculty will need assurances that the benefits merit the time they put into developing a portfolio (Robinson 1993).

Second, the support and cooperation of colleagues is critical to the success of any portfolio project (Blackburn and Pitney 1988; J.P. Murray 1994b; Seldin and Annis 1990). The development of a portfolio involves significant risks for the developer. He or she may discover imperfections, deficiencies, and attitudes he or she never suspected. It also means displaying one's warts to colleagues and chair. The risks are significant and should never be taken if one is not in a supportive, collegial relationship with one's colleagues. Although it is an individual's portfolio, it is the result of a group effort. When petty jealousies, backbiting, and grudges rule the department, the risks inherent in developing a portfolio unquestionably outweigh the benefits. Colleagues need to be more than simply neutral; they must be supportive and cooperative.

"In practice, the well-knit portfolio usually represents collegial efforts. Most people need help from some 'other'— a teaching improvement specialist, a faculty colleague, or a department chair—to structure the portfolio and decide what goes in it" (Seldin and Annis 1990, p. 198). At many steps along the way, faculty will need the assistance of a "colleague," someone who can share their ideas, hopes, fears, successes, and failures and someone who can offer suggestions and feedback. This person needs to be a colleague in the sense of an "associate" or a "fellow traveler" rather than one who judges in the tradition of a peer evaluator.

Although support from colleagues across the campus is important, the support of departmental colleagues is indispensable.

> *Portfolio development and use must be situated in departments for disciplinary reasons as well. Epistemologies differ across disciplines, and so do fundamental ideas about teaching. It is important for colleagues within the same discipline to grapple with issues of what constitutes effective teaching in their field* (Cerbin 1994, p. 102).

Moreover, at universities and senior colleges, faculty members' loyalty is first to their discipline and second to their university. Even at community colleges where loyalty to one's discipline is less, faculty tend to respect the opinions of departmental or divisional colleagues over those of administrators—especially with regard to matters of teaching. And legitimate differences exist among disciplines that affect the definition of good teaching.

It should be noted, however, that faculty seeking mentors to assist them with the development of a portfolio need not look exclusively within their own discipline. Despite the issues of loyalty and differences in teaching objectives between disciplines, it can be argued that someone from another discipline can still be an effective mentor. In fact, someone from outside one's own discipline may find it easier to focus on teaching than on content (Annis 1993).

Third, all college and university administrators, including the president, must provide enthusiastic and public support. Adequate resources are a necessity (Blackburn and Pitney 1988). The improvement of teaching must become an institutional priority supported by top administrative officers (Cross 1993; Green 1990; Kremer, Malik, and Hazer 1993; Seldin 1993b; Stevenson 1995). "Significant change simply does not happen unless the people who work in an institution understand that the chief executive officer and the college's leadership are committed to that change" (McCabe and Jenrette 1990, pp. 194–95).

Moreover, administrative support is a necessary condition for implementing changes to any performance appraisal system, especially portfolios because they depart radically from the traditional evaluation systems (Blackburn and Pitney 1988; Seldin 1993b; Seldin and Annis 1991–92). An attitude of trust must exist between faculty and administration (Blackburn and Pitney 1988). "Administrators must vigorously and publicly commit themselves to the portfolio concept and provide the necessary financial support" (Seldin 1993b, p. 91). Administrators must be made to understand that for teaching portfolios to be effective, it is necessary that they surrender some control over evaluation and evaluation standards to the faculty. Some administrators will need to be reassured that individualizing the process of evaluation will not result in faculty members' slick presentations of slim products. It is not possible to present the appearance of good teaching if the evidence does not exist (Seldin 1992).

Although support for teaching portfolios must come from the president, deans, and academic vice presidents, the key players in this process are department chairs (J.P. Murray 1995b). Chairs and other "first-line" administrators may need education or training to be thoroughly familiar with the concept and the purposes of teaching portfolios (Eison 1993; Kremer, Malik, and Hazer 1993; Seldin 1993b). The importance of providing training for administrators *before* implementing the assessment of teaching portfolios can be illustrated by two very different experiences at two higher education institutions—a successful effort to introduce portfolios at a large community college (McCabe and Jenrette 1990) and a failed effort at a university (Robinson 1993). A salient difference is that, at the community college, administrators were provided extensive and thorough training before faculty created portfolios. At the university, administrators received no training, before or after faculty developed portfolios.

Administrators need to communicate that they and the institution are committed to the project. Commitment means that the result of a portfolio will mean something. It does not always mean that any and all efforts will automatically be rewarded. In some cases, appropriate resources may need to be placed at the disposal of the faculty member or the chair for improvement or renewal. But if honest introspection or reflection about teaching is to occur, it all must be done without any potential harm to faculty members who willingly take a risk and develop a teaching portfolio. Administrators will find themselves walking a narrow line that allows them to support and encourage the development of portfolios but prevents them from taking unilateral action. Administrators must be trusting (sometimes almost blindly trusting) that the teacher and his or her departmental colleagues will "do the right thing."

Fourth, important to this endeavor is training graduate students to teach. It is time to introduce the pedagogy of teaching into the education and indoctrination of graduate students. For too long, graduate students have been educated to become researchers, i.e., clones of their professors. The truth of the matter is that few go on to become researchers of note, but many go on to teach. Nearly half a century ago, Blegen and Cooper remarked, "The American college teacher is the only high-level professional . . . who enters upon a career with neither the prerequisite trail of competence nor experience in the use of the tools of his

But if honest introspection or reflection about teaching is to occur, it all must be done without any potential harm to faculty members who willingly take a risk and develop a teaching portfolio.

profession" (quoted in Seldin 1993b, p. 209). The typical newly minted Ph.D. is still thrust into the classroom without any formal education in teaching and must learn by trial and error. Although many become adequate teachers and some even become good teachers, they do so on their own. The sad part of this on-the-job training is that it is unnecessary. Every university engaged in educating graduate students has adequate resources to provide structured experiences that could benefit those who go on to teaching positions in higher education. A few universities are awakening to this need and creating programs to develop graduate students' teaching skills (see, e.g., Centra 1993 for a description of such a project at Syracuse University). Unfortunately, these programs are few and far between and often not part of the requirements for a doctorate. When they are not required, advisers (some of whom often express disdain for "pedagogy courses") will not urge their graduate students to take them. And without such encouragement, graduate students will not bother. Universities should strongly consider adding a "teaching component" to all graduate degrees, especially for master's-level programs, whose graduates tend to find positions teaching at community colleges.

Fifth, faculty need to feel ownership of the process (Green 1990; McCabe and Jenrette 1990; Seldin 1993b). Involving faculty in the decision-making process is a necessary condition for the success of any innovation in higher education. In addition to higher education's strong cultural bias toward shared governance, researchers reassure us that "participation tends to produce acceptance and joint ownership over . . . [a] decision" (Vroom and Jago 1988, p. 57). An unsuccessful attempt to introduce teaching portfolios to three departments at Old Dominion University was partly the result of not involving the faculty in the planning process before portfolios were introduced (Robinson 1993).

Faculty, in particular, should be involved in developing the criteria for evaluating the quality of teaching (Kremer, Malik, and Hazer 1993) and for assessing the quality of the portfolio. "Before any thought is given to professional portfolio construction, scholars should clearly understand what their institutions expect of them in terms of professional work and what evidence of successful performance is deemed appropriate" (Froh, Gray, and Lambert 1993, p. 106).

Faculty also need clear guidance on how to develop a portfolio and what might go into it (Seldin 1992), and failure to provide such guidance can spell disaster for a campus portfolio project (Robinson 1993). "Some institutions have found it helpful to make available portfolio models of exemplary, satisfactory, and unsatisfactory quality" (Seldin 1992, p. 14).

Sixth, a key component to making teaching a prominent and valued component of a college's or university's culture is the establishment of an effective and respected faculty development program (Green 1990; Rice and Austin 1990; Seldin 1993b). It is simply insufficient to promote excellence in teaching without providing a means for faculty to gain the understandings and skills needed to become effective teachers.

Summary

Criticisms of the academy recently have increased in intensity and attracted unwanted attention from state legislators, and a number of state legislatures have passed or are considering passing laws that would regulate colleges and universities. Attempts to legislate the number of courses a professor must teach, the size of classes, and time spent with students have become increasingly intense. These misguided efforts arise, in part, out of a misunderstanding of what teaching entails, but the criticisms also arise out of a growing belief that teaching is neither a priority nor done well at universities and colleges. Much of the criticism is coming from within the academy. Clearly, higher education officials must take such criticisms seriously and attempt to elevate teaching to a status equal to that now enjoyed by research. Teaching portfolios provide administrators with a means to start this process.

A critical first step to introducing teaching portfolios to college or university faculty is understanding the culture of that institution. The reward structure of colleges and universities clearly encourages professors to neglect teaching in favor of research; the dominance of the research culture is partly the result of the difficulty in objectively evaluating teaching. Most colleges and universities presently rely on computer-scored student evaluations of faculty. Such evaluations, however, tend to measure the common denominators of teaching and neglect the differences resulting from discipline, institutional mission, students' goals, and so on. Again, teaching portfolios provide administrators with a means to individualize the evaluation of teaching.

College administrators must take several actions to change the culture of a college or university. First, they must convince faculty that teaching portfolios will benefit them. Second, they must get colleagues to support one another. Third, all college administrators, including the president, must provide strong vocal and public support for the concept. Fourth, administrators must attempt to alter the way graduate students are socialized into the teaching profession. Fifth, administrators must give faculty ownership of the process. Sixth, administrators must establish an effective and respected faculty development program.

THE ROLE OF DEPARTMENT CHAIRS

If colleges and universities wish to alter their culture to value excellence in teaching, they must start with department chairs. Colleges and universities are organizations where "the power for decision making lies at the bottom rather than the top" (Fife 1982). Departments set the course for a university by means of the decisions they make. By deciding whom to hire, whom to grant tenure, and whom to promote, departments create the values of an institution. A department that denies tenure to an excellent teacher with a mediocre publishing record sends the clear and distinct message to all untenured junior faculty that teaching counts less than research.

It has almost been taken for granted that the quality of a university or college is determined by the quality of its departments. "Almost all will agree that the stature of individual departments largely determines the stature of the institution" (Bennett 1983, p. 52). Accordingly, the success of a college or university in achieving its mission depends heavily on the willingness of its academic departments to buy into the institutional mission. Therefore, those interested in achieving and sustaining excellence in education need to begin at the departmental level. "The likelihood of getting faculty involved in the improvement effort and generating strong interest in both process and the outcomes is greater where they are more likely to share interests, values, perspectives, and responsibilities. Thus . . . efforts to examine and strengthen educational quality are optimally conducted at the department level" (Hartnett 1975, p. 61).

The Importance of Department Chairs

If the quality of academic departments is vital to the well-being of colleges and universities, then the quality of departmental leadership is critical. In fact, "the most powerful predictor of organizational effectiveness in colleges and universities is administrative behavior. Results from . . . research show that administrators are more important than environment, structure, age, institution type, and control in accounting for performance" (Whetten and Whetten 1985, pp. 35–36).

If an organization's effectiveness largely depends on administrative behavior, it seems reasonable that chairs, by virtual of their sheer numbers, are key players—an estimated 50,000+ department chairs in four-year colleges and universities alone (Gmelch and Miskin 1993). If two-year colleges

are included, the number nearly doubles. In all, it is likely that chairs outnumber all other administrators by five to one. And because much of the power within higher education institutions rests in departments, it also seems reasonable to conclude that chairs are key players. Therefore, when attempting to develop a culture that values and rewards excellence in teaching, the most important administrator within a college or university is the department chair. "An institution can run for a long time with an inept president but not for long with inept chairpersons" (Peltason 1984, p. xi). Moreover, the importance of departmental leadership is no less critical for two-year colleges than for four-year colleges.

> *The success of individual community colleges in the decades ahead will depend upon their ability to respond quickly to the educational needs of their service area with relevant, high-quality instruction furnished via a flexible delivery system—and at a competitive cost. Given this charge and the organizational chart of a typical community college, any beginning student of organizational behavior would quickly point to the first-level supervisor, the department/division head, as a key determinant in the future of the community college* (Hammons 1984, p. 14).

Research strongly supports the conclusion that the department chair is the essential player in creating and sustaining a departmental culture that supports and encourages excellence in teaching. Based on interviews with over 300 faculty from eight institutions, "the chair may well represent the single most important factor in determining whether or not a department actively supports teaching," and an effective and determined chair can significantly affect and cause "revolutionary changes" within a departmental culture that does not value teaching (Massey, Wilger, and Colbeck 1994, p. 17).

Characteristics of Excellent Departments
An investigation of the features that "constrain faculty in their ability to work together on teaching" (Massey, Wilger, and Colbeck 1994, p. 11) and characteristics of "departments that support effective teaching" (p. 14) identified three factors that hinder or prevent departments from creating a cul-

ture that holds excellence in teaching in high regard (see table 9). Interestingly, the research-versus-teaching dichotomy is only part of the reason that excellence in teaching is not valued at some institutions. In fact, excellence in research and excellence in teaching are equally respected and expected at some colleges and universities.

TABLE 9

Departmental Features Supporting or Constraining Effective Teaching

Features Constraining Faculty in Their Ability to Work Together on Teaching	Characteristics of Departments that Support Effective Teaching
Fragmented communication patterns that isolate faculty and prevent them from interacting around issues of undergraduate education	Frequent interaction among the faculty
	Tolerance of differences
	Generational equity
Tight resources that limit opportunities and strain faculty relationships	Workload equity
	Course rotation
Prevailing methods of evaluation and reward that undermine attempts to create an environment more conducive to faculty interaction	

Source: Adapted from Massey, Wilger, and Colbeck 1994.

"Reward structures offer only a partial explanation for the lack of effective undergraduate teaching. Of equal importance are broader questions about the organizational context within which undergraduate teaching occurs" (Massey, Wilger, and Colbeck 1994, p. 11). Foremost among the factors that negatively affect a department's culture in valuing excellence in teaching is "fragmented communication patterns" (p. 11). Five organizational elements contribute to dysfunctional communications in a department—autonomy, specialization, lack of civility, generational splits, and personal politics (Massey, Wilger, and Colbeck 1994)—and each one causes departmental faculty to avoid talking among themselves about any substantive issues, including the improvement of teaching.

On the other hand, "exemplary departments are distinguished by [a] supportive culture for undergraduate teaching, frequent interaction among faculty, tolerance of differences, generational equity, workload equity, and course rotation. Also important are peer as well as serious student teaching evaluation, balanced incentives, consensus decision making, and, above all, effective department chairs" (Massey, Wilger, and Colbeck 1994, p. 14). Although these features of exemplary departments certainly entail more, at heart they all point to effective and frequent communications among departmental members—in a word, "collegiality." "Collegial organizations emphasize consensus, shared power, consultation, and collective responsibilities—communities in which status differences are deemphasized and individuals interact as equals. Members of collegial organizations share aspirations and commitments, have frequent face-to-face interaction, and use civil discourse" (Massey, Wilger, and Colbeck 1994, p. 18).

The Chair and Leadership
Collegiality must be deliberately and carefully constructed; it does not happen without conscientious and deliberate leadership. Department chairs must provide that leadership; however, leadership in the academy takes a different shape from what it might take in other types of organizations. Collegiate faculty value their independence and their shared responsibility—a paradox that means colleges and universities require leaders who can facilitate the work of others without imposing a structure that stifles that work.

> *The ability of the formal office holders to exercise their leadership depends upon the ongoing support or compliance of other leaders and those being led. In such a situation, the leadership roles of those in formal positions of organizational authority could more appropriately be seen as those who facilitate or empower rather than those who control* (Seagren, Creswell, and Wheeler 1993, p. 21).

It would be a mistake, however, to assume that a chair

cannot be both a facilitator and a leader. Chairs can set a course for an academic department—what some call a mission statement (Diamond 1995) and others a vision (Cameron and Ulrich 1986; Creswell, Wheeler, Seagren, Egly, and Beyer 1990; Gmelch and Miskin 1993; Seagren, Creswell, and Wheeler 1993). But to achieve that vision, they must bring others along with them. In the jargon of leadership studies, this ability is called "transformational leadership."

As the name implies, transformational leadership involves a process of fundamental change. This change results in a new way of interpreting reality, in a different set of motives, in a higher vision of possibilities, not merely in the implementation of alternative actions or plans. It is as much concerned with helping people think differently about the problems they face as it is with creating solutions for those problems. It is as much the management of meaning as it is the management of substance (Cameron and Ulrich 1986, p. 12).

Creating Change

Chairs who desire to transform the culture of the department in ways that celebrate excellence in teaching should pay close attention to process as well as to leadership style. The process of change involves five stages:

1. Creating readiness;
2. Overcoming resistance;
3. Articulating a vision;
4. Generating commitment;
5. Institutionalizing implementation (Cameron and Ulrich 1986, p. 13).

In many ways, the process of transforming a department to value teaching boils down to two necessary skills for chairs: communicator and facilitator. Change agents with excellent communication skills can collaborate with faculty to shape a vision for the department. Numerous studies have consistently found that effective and respected chairs possess excellent interpersonal communication skills (Creswell et al. 1990; J.P. Murray 1992).

Skilled communication and facilitation skills enhance a chair's ability to create readiness, overcome resistance, and

The process of transforming a department to value teaching boils down to two necessary skills for chairs: communicator and facilitator.

generate commitment, and thus effectively generate meaningful change. In creating readiness, chairs would be wise to take the time to build consensus (Creswell et al. 1990; J.P. Murray 1993). Building a consensus for change takes time, and for change to be more than a transitory blip in the history of a department, it is absolutely necessary to take that time. Faculty will not assist in bringing about change and may even resist change if they do not believe in the outcome.

The key to transforming a department is the creation and articulation of a common vision. While chairs must be the individuals who articulate and doggedly promote the vision, they should not unilaterally create the vision.

> *Vision is the means by which a chair can create a focus or agenda for the department's current and future plans. The chair does not invent a vision and then attempt to impose it on disbelieving colleagues; rather, the chair facilitates the debate and discussion through which the department clarifies its options and becomes aware of its possibilities. The chair then oversees the strategies by which those fragments of a future are crystallized into a shared set of goals and a plan by which to reach them* (Seagren, Creswell, and Wheeler 1993, p. 20).

Academics often distrust administrators and, above all else, value participation in the decision-making process (J.P. Murray 1992, 1993). These two characteristics of faculties spell doom to any chair with the temerity to skip consensus building. According to a participant in a national study of excellent department chairs, "Don't do anything your faculty did not initiate. Remember the bubble-up theory—nothing should be done that doesn't come from the faculty" (Creswell et al. 1990, p. 24).

Such advice should not be construed to mean that the chair cannot help form the bubble or clear obstacles for fragile bubbles to percolate to the top. Excellent department chairs provide what another participant of the study called "atmospheric guidance" (Creswell et al. 1990, p. 32). And excellent communication skills are essential for atmospheric guidance. The research demonstrates that chairs judged excellent by their peers are seen as excellent communicators (Creswell et al. 1990; J.P. Murray 1992, 1993).

Once a chair decides to articulate a vision of excellence in teaching, it becomes necessary to determine a starting point. In reality, several starting points are likely, each needing different approaches. Ideally, the best place to begin is the hiring process. Any chair who can start by hiring a number of new faculty would have tremendous power to shape the future of the department. Unfortunately, most college and university chairs do not have this opportunity: Most chairs inherit existing departments with existing departmental cultures. Therefore, to facilitate change, chairs must develop support among the existing faculty. No one thing can be more disastrous to a chair who is attempting to set a new course for the department than ignoring an entrenched culture.

Existing departments are likely to include faculty at various stages in their careers. Most chairs will have the opportunity to hire some new faculty and to work with some recent hires striving for tenure, some midcareer faculty, and some senior faculty. Among these groups, chairs will find some enthusiastic faculty, some apathetic faculty, some stars, some duds, some bitter and hostile faculty, and some highly respected "gatekeeper" faculty. A wise chair will take time to learn who belongs to which category and develop strategies for involving each cluster in the development of a culture that values excellent teaching; the foolish one who neglects the needs of these groups will fail. The following suggestions will help chairs collaborate with all faculty, especially new faculty, influential or gatekeeper faculty, and burnt-out or hostile faculty.

Using rewards to improve teaching

Organizations tend to rely heavily on rewards to motivate workers. In higher education, however, rewards, although potentially effective, are often given to too few too rarely and consequently often become disincentives. Chairs at most institutions have very few rewards—tenure, promotion, and perhaps merit pay—they can dispense. The opportunity to award tenure comes once. The opportunity to award promotion comes at most three times. Consequently, these type of rewards are likely to have little effect on a faculty member's motivation.

Merit pay provokes passionate reactions among faculty and could work against the collegiality necessary for a culture of excellence in teaching to flourish in a department. "On some—perhaps many—campuses, merit pay tends to promote a decline in faculty collegiality and an increase in faculty hostility" (Altman 1993, p. 31). Moreover, because merit pay tends to reward recent behaviors over long-term behaviors, any changes motivated by merit pay could turn out to be short-lived phenomena. And "research studies have demonstrated that when you are rewarded for what you previously did for fun, you are less likely to choose that activity when the rewards cease. You come to expect that you should be paid" (McKeachie 1979, pp. 4–5).

Although chairs may not be able to give out large rewards, they may have smaller incentives at their disposal, and they should consider using them to encourage excellence in teaching. Often a small gesture coming from the right person at the right time is more appreciated than a "large" reward. An extremely effective and cost-conscious reward is simply recognition of accomplishments (Altman 1993; Lucas 1994; Pendleton-Parker and Parker 1993). Chairs should make every effort to see that faculty are recognized for their efforts, within both the department and the institution. A simple note of congratulations—perhaps with a copy on a departmental bulletin board—often pleases people. When a student compliments a departmental member's teaching, ask the student to write a short note to that effect and pass it on. Everyone likes to know that his or her accomplishments are valued.

Chairs often have a small pot of money available for their own travel or incidental departmental expenses. They could consider providing faculty with additional travel funds—especially for attending conferences dealing with teaching in higher education (Altman 1993; Lucas 1994). Chairs could also pay dues to professional organizations that promote teaching and for subscriptions to professional journals that deal with teaching and learning (Pendleton-Parker and Parker 1993). (See Cashin and Clegg 1994 for a comprehensive list of both general and discipline-specific professional journals related to teaching.)

Chairs might consider providing faculty who work to improve their teaching with additional clerical assistance in the form of a graduate assistant (Altman 1993) or a work-study student. Because faculty's most vocal complaint often involves parking, chairs might want to consider asking the administration to designate a free parking space to the "professor of the month" (Altman 1993). The chair might want to use some budget money to take a faculty member to lunch or even invite the faculty member and spouse to dinner.

An unusual and tantalizing suggestion is that departments create in-house visiting lecturers (Bevan 1985). By selecting one of their own to be a resource person for others, faculty recognize that person's contributions to the department. The chair may wish to make a faculty member widely respected for his or her teaching ability a "visiting" teacher for a semester. In return for a reduced teaching load, that person could guest in other's classes. It would not only reward the guest lecturer, but also provide other faculty with a role model. Chairs could provide some faculty with an internal sabbatical leave (Altman 1993), which could be useful to a faculty member trying to develop a new teaching strategy. An internal sabbatical leave could also be useful to a faculty member who needs to prepare publications for tenure or promotion but who has neglected research for teaching.

Some (including one of the anonymous reviewers of this manuscript) have suggested that chairs use their power to assign office space, courses, classrooms, and class meeting times for rewarding deserving faculty. Using such environmental conditions to reward some, however, will likely breed resentment in others, and rather than appearing to reward the deserving, such actions could seem like punishment to those deemed undeserving. In this case, it will be difficult, if not impossible, to build the desired collegiality.

Rewards are effective for faculty who are already doing an excellent job, but chairs also find it necessary to motivate faculty who are less enthusiastic about their teaching. Setting goals is an effective strategy for working with faculty at any stage of a career (Lucas 1994), and setting specific goals can be a compelling motivator (Latham and Yukl 1975). When the individual accepts them, the more difficult the goal, the greater the likelihood that it will be accomplished (Mento, Steel, and Karren 1987). Moreover, setting difficult goals and providing feedback on the individual's progress toward meeting the goals increases effectiveness (with self-generated feedback more effective than feedback from others [Ivancevich and McMahon 1982]). When it comes to whether setting goals is more effective when the goals are established by the faculty member, by the chair, or mutually by both, the research literature is decidedly undecided (Robbins 1989). Several factors suggest, however, that when dealing with academic professionals, the process of setting goals should be participative. First, the probability of difficult goals' being attained is definitely increased when the faculty member accepts the goal. Second, professors expect and demand a great deal of autonomy in determining the conduct of their work. Third, the academy has a long tradition of participation in governance; therefore, it is much more probable that goals selected with the advice and consent of the faculty member will be attained.

Mutually determined goals also enhance the opportunity to become the self-directed, reflective practitioners teaching portfolios provide. "To develop goals and action steps, individuals become reflective practitioners and devote energy to thinking about a direction for their lives" (Lucas 1994, p. 84). One of the greatest advantages of teaching portfolios is that they place control of one's professional life in one's own hands. In other words, they empower faculty to become professional educators and to define it in their own terms. Setting goals and measuring success in attaining them through use of a teaching portfolio enables one to take charge of his or her life.

The role of the chair in setting goals is to delineate clearly departmental and institutional expectations. The chair should also assist faculty in making goals realistic, concrete, and measurable (Lucas 1994). If faculty are to succeed, they must set attainable goals. Idealistic faculty—particularly new faculty (Boice 1991)—often believe that they can attain much more than circumstances allow. Faculty need to set goals that can be measured; vague goals create complacency and disillusionment. A goal "to increase scholarly productivity" is much more likely to go unmet than a goal "to submit one manuscript by the end of the semester." A goal "to use cooperative learning techniques more often" is much more likely to go unmet than a goal "to develop and test five cooperative learning assignments before the end of the semester." Moreover, the successful attainment of that goal will motivate the faculty to achieve other goals.

Chairs should assist faculty by enabling self-monitored feedback. They might consider providing the faculty member with a self-evaluation checklist that breaks goals down into logical steps. As individuals are motivated by success, each time a faculty member can note that he or she accomplished one of the steps, the feeling of successful accomplishment will motivate him or her to start the next step.

A critical step in developing a culture that promotes excellence in teaching is to establish an atmosphere of collegiality. Collegiality depends heavily on trust, and trust starts with communication. "Lack of information provokes charges of not being consulted or of being manipulated, resulting in failure to enlist sufficient faculty and administrative support" (Bevan 1985, p. 55). Chairs can begin to create an atmosphere of trust by communicating everything that is not confidential (Pendleton-Parker and Parker 1993). Several research studies demonstrate that department members value being kept informed very highly even when the information does not seem to directly affect them (J.P. Murray 1992). For comprehensive communications to occur, chairs should maintain an open-door policy—although simply saying that your door is always open is not enough. The chair must be a sincere listener and must act upon faculty members' requests—even if the only action is to tell them that no action is possible (Pendleton-Parker and Parker 1993). And the chair cannot wait for faculty to come to his or her office: A chair must make certain to visit faculty (especially difficult faculty) in *their* offices (Bevan 1985; Boice 1993).

Faculty expect department chairs to communicate departmental needs to higher-level administrators. Faculty also sincerely value chairs who actively promote the department's and faculty members' accomplishments to higher-level administrators (Bevan 1985; J.P. Murray 1992; Pendleton-Parker and Parker 1993).

Effective communications form the foundation to build a departmental culture that values excellence in teaching. Teaching will never be highly valued unless colleges and universities develop a culture where teaching becomes what Shulman calls "community property" and we create what Palmer calls "good talk about good teaching" (Astin 1993; J. Davis 1994; Edgerton 1993; Lucas 1994; Palmer 1993; Shulman 1993). Chairs must take the leadership in creating this culture.

Chairs can begin the good talk by setting time aside in every departmental meeting to discuss teaching (Lucas 1994). Rather than have such a discussion follow some contentious agenda item, it is probably more effective to start the meeting with a discussion of teaching. Chairs may want to consider setting aside one meeting a month or a semester to discuss nothing but issues related to teaching and curricula (Pendleton-Parker and Parker 1993). They may want to set up workshops on teaching (Lucas 1994), which could take the form of a faculty member's presentation on an innovation he or she found successful or the results of a classroom research project. A faculty member might want to research a teaching topic and present his or her findings—which can be quite effective when a faculty member identifies a weakness in his or her teaching and sets out to research solutions. To facilitate such efforts, chairs should consider setting up a departmental library that includes books on improving the effectiveness of teaching and newsletters about teaching.

Part of the "good talk about good teaching" requires chairs to get teaching colleagues to discuss each other's teaching. A chair might consider setting up a committee on the improvement of teaching that could assist the chair in creating a climate where faculty feel comfortable seeking help with teaching from one another and visiting one another's classes. To set the example, chairs should consider inviting faculty to observe and comment on their classes (Lucas 1994). Chairs may wish to recruit some of the best teachers to start the project.

Chairs who wish to encourage excellence in teaching can encourage faculty to present at and/or attend conferences dealing with teaching or at discipline conferences that sponsor teaching-related sessions. They can do so by circulating calls for papers and conference registration materials to faculty. Chairs might want to consider a bulletin board dedicated to teaching-related publications and conferences. A computer bulletin board and/or a voice-mail distribution list can also be quite effective means of promoting teaching-related conferences.

Chairs will find some faculty who have the respect of their departmental colleagues and tend to act as "gatekeepers." And they will find some difficult faculty who are embittered because of some real or imagined wrong. To succeed, chairs should woo and win over both groups. Some approaches are appropriate for both groups, others for only one. Chairs wishing to encourage the development of teaching portfolios as a means of improving teaching would be wise to solicit a small number of the gatekeepers who also have reputations for being excellent teachers to experiment with and develop model teaching portfolios.

Hiring new faculty

Chairs can have the greatest effect on a department's culture by exercising their influence in the hiring of new faculty. When hiring new faculty, it is important to determine the fit between the candidate and the institution (Pendleton-Parker and Parker 1993). Some departmental cultures could cause a potential "star" to quickly burn out and self-destruct. A new hire will have little opportunity to thrive in a department with a cynical and bitter culture of personal rivalries. A new faculty member hired because of his or her potential to become an excellent teacher may fail to achieve tenure in a department that values research. "Fit" involves the aspirations of both the department and the candidate.

To create a culture that expects excellence in teaching, chairs need to stress the importance of good teaching during the process of interviewing candidates. A chair wishing to emphasize the importance of teaching should ask potential candidates to provide evidence of excellence in teaching, and finalists should be asked to teach a class or two during their interview (Lucas 1994). Although observing a candidate teach can help a committee make a decision, the classes should have real students and the candidate should be given ample time to prepare. It is highly unlikely that candidates will do their best if they are ill-informed about what students are studying.

Once a new faculty member is hired, the chair should make certain that the faculty member has every chance to succeed. Often in higher education, we simply tell new faculty what course they are to teach and where they meet. Research on how new faculty acclimate to their roles clearly shows that providing mentoring, especially informal and voluntary, is very effective (Lucas 1994; Pendleton-Parker and Parker 1993). Chairs wishing to encourage new faculty to become excellent teachers should consider pairing them with senior faculty who have earned reputations for excellence in teaching. New faculty should not become reliant on a single senior faculty member to the exclusion of other departmental members, however (Pendleton-Parker and Parker 1993).

To create a culture that expects excellence in teaching, chairs need to stress the importance of good teaching during the process of interviewing candidates.

Chairs should develop an ongoing relationship with new faculty. "Have as much chair/new faculty contact and evaluation—even if only informal over coffee or a beer—as possible; make sure hard decisions never come as a surprise" (Pendleton-Parker and Parker 1993, p. 205). Chairs can assist new faculty in adjusting their expectations to the reality of the department and the institution. Research demonstrates that most new faculty have unrealistic expectations about how to balance the demands of teaching and research (Boice 1991). At first, most new faculty tend to underestimate the amount of time teaching will take, and they often find it necessary to adjust and tend to overcompensate by spending too much time in preparation. Overpreparing, however, exacerbates the problem and causes new faculty to rely on dysfunctional teaching strategies.

New faculty who have realistic expectations exhibit a willingness to seek help from colleagues and instructional development specialists (Boice 1991); therefore, chairs may wish to make new faculty aware of the instructional development resources available on campus.

Dealing with difficult faculty

Chairs report that dealing with difficult faculty takes up a great deal of time and that their efforts are usually unsuccessful (Boice 1993; Lucas 1994). Once they have been established in a department, teaching portfolios offer an excellent vehicle for refocusing a faculty member on teaching. By encouraging a difficult faculty member to develop a portfolio, the chair can cause the individual to focus on teaching while also respecting the individual's autonomy. Moreover, the chair can communicate the message to the faculty member that he or she is a valuable contributor to the department. In some cases, that communication may be enough to bring the person back to the dedication to and enthusiasm for teaching he or she had at the start of the career.

Most chairs do not know what to do for difficult faculty members and tend to try to ignore the situation (Lucas 1994). Ignoring the situation, however, almost never succeeds, because it only heightens the individual's sense that he or she is being treated unjustly (Boice 1993). An effective solution is for chairs to "reach out to alienated members on a human level" (Lucas 1994, p. 92); simply being friendly and courteous to difficult faculty members could win them over (Boice 1993; Lucas 1994). The chair could make it a point to seek out difficult faculty members for small talk. Once contact at a human level is established, the chair then asks the faculty member why he or she is withdrawn and what it would take to motivate him or her to change. If rapport has been established, faculty members will be forthcoming, and the chair should "be prepared . . . to agree to some extent with the content of their complaints and criticisms" (Boice 1993, p. 135). The next step is to negotiate goals or a growth contract that is to result in changed behavior. When the effort is sincere, chairs report a "better relationship with the difficult faculty member, the individual's getting more involved or accepting more responsibility in the department, and the individual's making fewer abrasive comments at meetings" (Lucas 1994, p. 94).

Several other approaches are available to chairs working with difficult faculty members. The chair may request the difficult faculty member to team teach a course (Lucas 1994), which can be an effective way to introduce burned-out faculty to new teaching techniques. To work, however, chairs must assign their best teachers to team with those they want to help, and they must adjust teaching loads in a way that does not add to either team member's workload (usually by counting a team-taught class the same as an individually taught class). Exchange programs with nearby colleges and universities have been effective in introducing new ideas to a faculty with little turnover (J.P. Murray 1995a), and they can be especially effective with disgruntled or burned-out faculty (Lucas 1994).

Summary

If colleges and universities wish to alter their culture to value excellence in teaching, they must start with the department chair. It is no exaggeration to say that the quality of an institution depends directly on the quality of its department chairs. Effective department chairs facilitate the creation and promotion of a departmental vision. To accomplish it, chairs must be effective communicators and consensus builders. Chairs must learn to assist new faculty in learning their roles and find ways to help embittered and withdrawn faculty to once again become productive teachers. Both tasks require chairs to become creative in the ways they work with and reward faculty.

CONCLUSION

This monograph has argued that teaching portfolios are a means of effectively evaluating and improving teaching in higher education. The improvement of teaching and learning is a worthwhile objective if for no other reason than the moral obligation colleges and universities have to provide a quality education to their students. The improvement of teaching and learning is made all the more imperative by the increasing public cynicism over the value of a college education. College and university leaders are spending enormous amounts of time and energy fending off public criticism of the academy. In many cases, these criticisms are coming from legislators who can and have reduced funding to public colleges and universities.

A large part of the criticism stems from the belief that students, parents, and taxpayers are simply not getting their money's worth from higher education. While academic leaders can and do dismiss this concern as being a vulgar preoccupation with consumerism, these attacks have an effect. Moreover, it is perhaps true that colleges and universities have strayed from their mission as educational institutions. This monograph has argued that by introducing teaching portfolios, colleges and universities can not only rediscover their historical mission but also convince the public that higher education deserves the support it has traditionally enjoyed.

It is difficult to define teaching portfolios succinctly because the definition depends on the intended use, which varies. Colleges and universities have used teaching portfolios to meet four different needs. Portfolios can document excellence in teaching, empower professors to define quality teaching in their own terms, allow colleges and universities to demonstrate that teaching is an institutional priority, and individualize faculty development.

Because teaching portfolios allow individual faculty members to tailor the assessment of teaching and learning to their own beliefs, the content varies from one professor to another. It is important, however, that the minimum content be specified when portfolios are intended to be used for summative evaluation. Moreover, teaching portfolios should contain a statement of the professor's philosophy of teaching. The philosophical beliefs one holds consciously and unconsciously influence one's behavior. A professor's beliefs about the teaching and learning process directly influence his or her demeanor in the classroom, treatment of students, choices of teaching strategies, choices of assessment strategies, beliefs about grading, and so on. Unless these beliefs are made explicit, professors may never examine the validity of their beliefs and hence the value of their practices.

Because portfolios contain both quantitative and qualitative materials, they allow evaluators to get a view of a professor's teaching in the actual context of that teaching. Portfolios present a deeply woven, multilayered, richly varied picture of a professor's accomplishments in teaching. Because the context of teaching is firmly and inextricably interwoven throughout a teaching portfolio, its evaluation presents some specific challenges to campus administrators. These opportunities are analogous to the challenges that tenure and promotion committees grapple with when attempting to judge the quality of publications, teaching materials, syllabi, and so on. The key is to develop valid, reliable, and fair procedures and standards that fit with the institution's mission.

The essence of a teaching portfolio is the assessment of the teaching/learning process. Assessment requires that faculty gather data from self, students, and colleagues, which can be done through a variety of formal and informal ways. Gathering and analyzing data is a necessary, but not a sufficient, condition for teaching portfolios to impact one's teaching. For the data to affect teaching, one needs to reflect on what the data reveal about his or her teaching.

If teaching portfolios are to be used to improve teaching, campuses must define what they mean by "good teaching." The literature provides many and varied definitions—some contradicting others—because the definition of teaching depends a great deal on the institution's mission, the discipline, and the level of students' interest and preparation. But merely engaging a campus faculty in the discussion of how to define good teaching will have salutary benefits. Such discussion forces many to think about teaching in new ways, maybe for the first time.

This monograph has argued that higher education must undergo a cultural shift and become once again institutions that place teaching at the center of their being. If higher education's leaders shrink from this responsibility, it will be done for them by individuals much less qualified. The attacks on higher education are unlikely to subside if ignored, in part because society now believes higher education is the best ticket—maybe the only ticket—to a decent quality of life for their children and themselves. Even if the external pressures would disappear tomorrow, higher education should look at how its mission has become ambiguous and take this opportunity to refocus itself. Higher education should first and foremost be an educational organization, which means celebrating teaching and learning. Teaching portfolios are one means to accomplish that task.

REFERENCES

The Educational Resources Information Center (ERIC) Clearing-house on Higher Education abstracts and indexes the current litera-ture on higher education for inclusion in ERIC's database and an-nouncement in ERIC's monthly bibliographic journal, *Resources in Education* (RIE). Most of these publications are available through the ERIC Document Reproduction Service (EDRS). For publications cited in this bibliography that are available from EDRS, ordering number and price code are included. Readers who wish to order a publication should write to the ERIC Document Reproduction Service, 3900 Wheeler Avenue, Alexandria, Virginia 22304. (Phone orders with VISA or MasterCard are taken at 800/337-ERIC or 703/823-0500.) When ordering, please specify the document (ED) number. Documents are available as noted in microfiche (MF) and paper copy (PC). If you have the price code ready when you call, EDRS can quote an exact price. The last page of the latest issue of *Resources in Education* also has the current cost, listed by code.

Altman, H.B. 1993. *Rewarding Faculty Performance: What Can We Do When the Cupboard Is Almost Bare?* Proceedings of the Tenth Annual Conference of Academic Chairpersons: Selecting, Moti-vating, Evaluating, and Rewarding Faculty, February, Orlando, Florida.

American Association of University Professors. 1994. *The Work of Faculty: Expectations, Priorities, and Rewards.* Washington, D.C.: Committee C on College and University Teaching, Research, and Publication.

Angelo, T.A., and K.P. Cross. 1993. *Classroom Assessment Tech-niques: a Handbook for College Teachers.* 2d ed. San Francisco: Jossey-Bass.

Annis, L.F. 1993. "The Key Role of the Mentor." In *Successful Use of Teaching Portfolios,* edited by P. Seldin and Associates. Bolton, Mass.: Anker Publishing Co.

Astin, H.S. 1993. "Responsive Faculty or Responding to Student Needs." In *Faculty as Teachers,* edited by M. Weimer. University Park: Pennsylvania State Univ.

Barr, R.B. March 1995. "From Teaching to Learning: A New Reality for Community Colleges." *Leadership Abstracts* 83.

Bennett, J.B. 1983. "What Lies in the Future for Department Chair-persons?" *Educational Record* 64: 52–56.

Bernoff, R.A. 1992. "Effective Teaching Techniques: A Workshop." Paper presented at the National Conference on Successful College Teaching and Administration, March, Orlando, Florida.

Bevan, J.M. 1985. "Who Has the Role of Building in Incentives?" In *Incentives for Faculty Vitality,* edited by R.G. Baldwin. New Di-rections for Higher Education No. 51. San Francisco: Jossey-Bass.

Blackburn, R.T., and J.A. Pitney. 1988. *Performance Appraisal for Faculty: Implications for Higher Education*. Ann Arbor, Mich.: National Center for Research to Improve Postsecondary Teaching and Learning. ED 316 066. 59 pp. MF–01; PC–03.

Boice, R. 1991. "New Faculty as Teachers." *Journal of Higher Education* 62: 150–73.

———. 1993. "Coping with Difficult Colleagues." In *Enhancing Departmental Leadership,* edited by J.B. Bennett and D.J. Figui. New York: Oryx Press.

Boyer, E.L. 1990. *Scholarship Reconsidered: The Priorities of the Professorate*. Princeton, N.J.: Carnegie Foundation for the Advancement of Teaching. ED 326 149. 151 pp. MF–01; PC not available EDRS.

Braskamp, L.A., D.C. Brandenberg, and J.C. Ory. 1984. *Evaluating Teaching Effectiveness*. Beverly Hills, Calif.: Sage.

Braskamp, L.A., and J.C. Ory. 1994. *Assessing Faculty Work: Enhancing Individual and Institutional Performance*. Higher and Adult Education Series. San Francisco: Jossey-Bass. ED 368 305. 333 pp. MF–01; PC not available EDRS.

Brinko, K.T. 1993. "The Practice of Giving Feedback to Improve Teaching." *Journal of Higher Education* 64: 574–93.

Cage, M.C. 22 January 1995. "Regulating Faculty Workloads." *Chronicle of Higher Education:* A30+.

Cameron, K.S., and D.O. Ulrich. 1986. "Transformation Leadership in Colleges and Universities." In *Higher Education: Handbook of Theory and Research,* edited by J.C. Smart. Vol. 2. New York: Agathon Press.

Cashin, W.E, and V.L. Clegg. 1994. "Periodicals Related to College Teaching." Idea Paper No. 28. Rev. Manhattan: Kansas State Univ., Center for Faculty Evaluation and Development. HE 029 194. 4 pp. MF–01; PC–01.

Centra, J.A. 1992. *The Use of the Teaching Portfolio and the Student Instructional Report for Summative Evaluation*. SIR Report No. 6. Princeton, N.J.: Educational Testing Service.

———. 1993. *Reflective Faculty Evaluation*. San Francisco: Jossey-Bass.

Cerbin, W. 1994. "The Course Portfolio as a Tool for Continuous Improvement of Teaching and Learning." *Journal on Excellence in College Teaching* 5: 95–105.

Chickering, A.W., and Z.F. Gamson. 1987. "Seven Principles for Good Practice in Undergraduate Education." Milwaukee: Johnson Foundation. ED 319 293. 4 pp. MF–01 PC–01.

Clinic to Improve University Teaching. 1974. *Teaching Analysis by Students—TABS*. Amherst: Univ. of Massachusetts at Amherst.

Coffman, S.J. 1991. "Improving Your Teaching through Small-Group

Diagnosis." *College Teaching* 39: 80–82.

Cohen, P.A., and W.J. McKeachie. 1980. "The Role of Colleagues in the Evaluation of College Teaching." *Improving College and University Teaching* 28: 147–54.

Creswell, J.W., D.W. Wheeler, A.T. Seagren, N.J. Egly, and K.D Beyer. 1990. *The Academic Chairperson's Handbook.* Lincoln: Univ. of Nebraska Press.

Cross, K.P. 1990. "Teaching to Improve Learning." *Journal on Excellence in College Teaching* 1: 9–22.

———. 1993. "Classroom Assessment." In *Faculty as Teachers,* edited by M. Weimer. University Park: Pennsylvania State Univ.

Davis, B.G. 1993. *Tools for Teaching.* San Francisco: Jossey-Bass.

Davis, J.R. 1994. "Deepening and Broadening the Dialogue about Teaching." *To Improve the Academy* 13: 39–49. ED 392 385. 392 pp. MF–01; PC–16.

De Fillips, D.C. 1993. "Professional Portfolios: The York College Model for Faculty Development, Evaluation, and Rewards. Achievements and Aspirations: A Case Study." Unpublished manuscript. Jamaica, N.Y.: York College.

Diamond, R.M. 1995. "The Department Chair's Role in Unifying Institutional Priorities and Faculty Rewards." Paper presented at the Twelfth Annual Conference of Academic Chairpersons, February, Orlando, Florida.

Dillon, W.T., and D. Lieberman. Summer 1996. "Institutional Change and Departmental Decision Making: The Importance of Chairs' Perspectives." *The Department Chair: A Newsletter for Academic Administrators:* 2–3.

DuBois, G. 1993. "Hidden Characteristics of Effective Community College Teachers." *Community College Journal of Research and Practice* 17: 459–71.

Eble, K. 1988. *The Craft of Teaching.* San Francisco: Jossey-Bass.

Edgerton, R. 20 April 1988. "Melange." *Chronicle of Higher Education:* B2.

———. 1993. "The Reexamination of Faculty Priorities." *Change* 25: 10–22.

Edgerton, R., P. Hutchings, and K. Quinlan. 1991. *The Teaching Portfolio: Capturing the Scholarship of Teaching.* Washington, D.C.: American Association for Higher Education. ED 353 892. 62 pp. MF–01; PC not available EDRS.

Eison, J. 1993. "Setting the Stage: Introducing the Teaching Portfolio Concept to One's Campus." *Journal of Staff, Program, and Organizational Development* 11: 115–19.

Fairweather, J. 1993. "Faculty Rewards Reconsidered: The Nature of Tradeoffs." *Change* 25: 44–47.

Fayne, H.R. 1991. "Practicing What We Preach: Key Issues in Faculty Development." Paper presented at an annual meeting of the American Association of Colleges for Teacher Education, March, Atlanta, Georgia. ED 330 266. 45 pp. MF–01; PC–02.

Feldman, K.A. 1976. "The Superior College Teacher from the Students' View." *Research in Higher Education* 5: 243–88.

———. 1987. "Research Productivity and Scholarly Accomplishment of College Teachers as Related to Their Instructional Effectiveness: A Review and Exploration." *Research in Higher Education:* 26: 227–98.

Fennell, T. 1992. "Teaching Class: Research and Teaching by Professors." *Maclean's* 45: 56–59.

Fife, J. 1982. "Foreword." In *The Department Chair: Professional Development and Role Conflict,* by D.B. Booth. ASHE-ERIC Higher Education Report No. 10. Washington, D.C.: George Washington Univ., School of Education and Human Development. ED 226 689. 60 pp. MF–01; PC–03.

———. 1993. "Foreword." In *Enhancing Promotion, Tenure, and Beyond: Faculty Socialization as a Cultural Process,* by W.G. Tierney and R.A. Rhoads. ASHE-ERIC Higher Education Report No. 6. Washington, D.C.: George Washington Univ., School of Education and Human Development.

French-Lazovik, G. 1981. "Peer Review." In *Handbook of Teacher Evaluation,* edited by J. Millman. Newbury Park, Calif.: Sage.

Froh, C., P.J. Gray, and L.M. Lambert. 1993. "Representing Faculty Work: The Professional Portfolio." In *Recognizing Faculty Work: Reward Systems for the Year 2000,* edited by R.M. Diamond and B.E. Adam. New Directions for Higher Education No. 81. San Francisco: Jossey-Bass.

Fuhrmann, B.S., and A.F. Grasha. 1983. *A Practical Handbook for College Teachers.* Boston: Little, Brown.

Gardiner, L. 1994. *Redesigning Higher Education: Producing Dramatic Gains in Student Learning.* ASHE-ERIC Higher Education Report No. 7. Washington, D.C.: George Washington Univ., Graduate School of Education and Human Development. ED 394 441. 240 pp. MF–01; PC–10.

Gay, L.R. 1987. *Educational Research: Competencies for Analysis and Application.* Columbus, Ohio: Merrill Publishing Co.

Gmelch, W.H., and V.D Miskin. 1993. *Leadership Skills for Department Chairs.* Bolton, Mass.: Anker Publishing Co.

Goulden, N.R. 1991. "Improving Instructors' Speaking Skills." Idea Paper No. 24. Manhattan: Kansas State Univ. ED 339 052. 6 pp. MF–01; PC–01.

Grasha, A.F. 1990. "Using Traditional versus Naturalistic Approaches to Assessing Learning Styles in College Teaching." *Journal on Excellence in College Teaching* 1: 23–38.

Green, M.F. 1990. "Why Good Teaching Needs Active Leadership."

In *How Administrators Can Improve Teaching,* edited by P. Seldin and Associates. San Francisco: Jossey-Bass.

Hammons, J. 1984. "The Department/Division Chairperson: Educational Leader?" *Community and Junior College Journal* 54: 14–19.

Hart, K.A. 1989. "Faculty Performance Appraisal: A Recommendation for Growth and Change. Accent on Improving College Teaching and Learning." Ann Arbor, Mich.: National Center for Research to Improve Postsecondary Teaching and Learning. ED 329 148. 6 pp. MF–01; PC–01.

Hartnett, R.T. 1975. *Strengthening Institutional Quality through Institutional Research.* New Directions for Higher Education No. 12. San Francisco: Jossey-Bass.

Heller, S. 13 April 1988. "Miami-Dade College Begins Project to Bolster Teaching by Evaluating New Professors and Rewarding Classroom Performance." *Chronicle of Higher Education:* A17–A18.

Higgins, C.S., E.M. Hawthorne, J.A. Cape, and L. Bell, 1993. "The Successful Community College Instructor: A Profile for Recruitment." *Community College Review* 21: 27–36.

Higher Education Research Institute. 1991. *The American College Teacher: National Norms for the 1989–90 HERI Faculty Survey.* Los Angeles: Univ. of California. ED 351 906. 163 pp. MF–01; PC not available EDRS.

Hilsen, L., and L. Rutherford. 1991. "Front Line Faculty Development: Chairs Constructively Critiquing Colleagues in the Classroom." *To Improve the Academy* 10: 251–69. ED 392 383. 278 pp. MF–01; PC–12.

Hoover, K.H. 1980. *College Teaching Today: A Handbook for Postsecondary Instruction.* Boston: Allyn & Bacon.

Howe, F., and J. Moran. 1995. "A Collaborative Approach to Professional Development." *Teaching Today* 1(1): 5.

"In Box." 17 March 1995. *Chronicle of Higher Education:* A16.

Ivancevich, J.M., and J.T. McMahon. 1982. "The Effects of Goal Setting, External Feedback, and Self-Generated Feedback on Outcome Variables: A Field Experiment." *Academy of Management Journal* 25: 359–72.

Kahn, S. 1993. "Better Teaching through Better Evaluation: A Guide for Faculty and Institutions." *To Improve the Academy* 12: 111–26. ED 392 384. 288 pp. MF–01; PC–12.

Katz, J. 1989. "Turning Professors into Teachers." *Journal of Staff, Program, and Organization Development* 7: 3–6.

Keig, L., and M.D. Waggoner. 1994. *Collaborative Peer Review: The Role of Faculty in Improving College Teaching.* ASHE-ERIC Higher Education Report No. 2. Washington, D.C.: George Washington Univ., Graduate School of Education and Human Development. ED 378 925. 193 pp. MF–01; PC–08.

Kogut, L.S. 1984. "Quality Circles: A Japanese Management Technique for the Classroom." *Improving College and University Teaching* 32: 123–27.

Kremer, J.F., D.J. Malik, and J.T. Hazer. 1993. "Teaching Effectiveness: Assessment and Rewards." Paper presented at the Tenth Annual Conference of Academic Chairpersons, February, Orlando, Florida.

Latham, G.P., and G.A. Yukl. 1975. "A Review of Research on the Application of Goal Setting in Organizations." *Academy of Management Journal* 18: 824–45.

Lowman, J. 1984. *Mastering the Techniques of Teaching*. San Francisco: Jossey-Bass.

Lucas, A.F. 1994. *Strengthening Departmental Leadership*. San Francisco: Jossey-Bass.

———. Summer 1996. "Quality Departments: Surveillance or Accountability?" *The Department Chair: A Newsletter for Academic Administrators:* 1+.

McCabe, R.H., and M.S. Jenrette. 1990. "Leadership in Action: A Campuswide Effort to Strengthen Teaching." In *How Administrators Can Improve Teaching,* edited by P. Seldin and Associates. San Francisco: Jossey-Bass.

McKeachie, W.J. 1979. "Perspectives from Psychology: Financial Incentives Are Ineffective for Faculty." In *Academic Rewards in Higher Education,* edited by D.R. Lewis and W.E. Becker. Cambridge, Mass.: Ballinger Publishing Co.

———. 1986. *Teaching Tips.* Lexington, Mass.: D.C. Heath.

McKeachie, W.J., Y.G. Lin, M. Daugherty, M.M. Moffett, C. Neigler, J. Nork, M. Walz, and R. Baldwin. 1980. "Using Student Ratings Consultation to Improve Instruction." *British Journal of Educational Psychology* 50: 168–74.

Massey, W.F., A.K. Wilger, and C. Colbeck. July/August 1994. "Departmental Cultures and Teaching Quality: Overcoming 'Hollowed' Collegiality." *Change* 26: 11–20.

Meacham, J. May 1993. "Class Dismissed: Universities Should Start Caring about How Well—How Much—Teachers Teach." *Washington Monthly:* 42–46.

Mento, A.J., R.P. Steel, and R.J. Karren. 1987. "A Meta-analytic Study of Effects of Goal Setting on Task Performance: 1966–1984." *Organizational Behavior and Human Decision Process* 39: 52–83.

Miller, R.I. 1987. *Evaluating Faculty for Promotion and Tenure*. San Francisco: Jossey-Bass.

Millis, B.J. 1991. "Putting the Teaching Portfolio in Context." *To Improve the Academy* 10: 215–29. ED 392 383. 278 pp. MF–01; PC–12.

Murray, H.G. 1987. "Acquiring Student Feedback That Improves Instruction." In *Teaching Large Classes Well,* edited by M.G.

Weimer. New Directions for Teaching and Learning No. 32. San Francisco: Jossey-Bass.

Murray, J.I. 1994. *A Holistic, Collaborative Approach to Teaching Assessment Instructional Development.* ED 367 386. 31 pp. MF–01; PC–02.

Murray, J.P. 1 November 1991. "Participative Evaluation." *Innovation Abstracts:* 2.

———. 1992. "Expectations of Department Chairpersons: A Delphi Case Study." *Journal of Staff, Program, and Organization Development* 10: 13–21.

———. 1993. "The Department Chairperson: The Confessions of a Researcher Turned Practitioner." *Journal of Staff, Program, and Organization Development* 11: 79–88.

———. October 1994a. "Portfolios: Classroom Moments Frozen in Time." *Academic Leader:* 1–3.

———. 1994b. "Why Teaching Portfolios?" *Community College Review* 22: 33–43.

———. 1995a. "Faculty Misdevelopment in Ohio Two-Year Colleges." *Community College Journal of Research Practice* 19: 549–63.

———. 1995b. "The Teaching Portfolio: A Tool for Department Chairpersons to Create a Climate of Teaching Excellence." *Innovative Higher Education* 19: 163–75.

National Center on Postsecondary Teaching, Learning, and Assessment. Winter 1993. "How Devalued Is Teaching?" *Newsletter:* 1–2.

O'Neil, C., and A. Wright. 1992. *Recording Teaching Accomplishment: A Dalhousie Guide to the Teaching Dossier.* 3d ed. Halifax, Nova Scotia: Dalhousie Univ.

Ory, J.C. 1991. "Changes in Teaching in Higher Education." *Instructional Evaluation* 11: 1–9.

Overall, J.U., and H.W. Marsh. 1979. "Midterm Feedback from Students: Its Relationship to Instructional Improvement and Students' Cognitive Affective Outcomes." *Journal of Educational Psychology* 71: 856–65.

Palmer, P.J. 1993. "Good Talk about Good Teaching: Improving Teaching through Conversation and Community." *Change* 25: 8–14.

Peltason, J.W. 1984. "Foreword." In *Chairing the Academic Department: Leadership among Peers,* by A. Tucker. 2d ed. New York: Macmillan.

Pendleton-Parker, B., and S. Parker. 1993. "Perceptions of Motivation, Evaluation, and Rewards for Faculty for the 21st Century: Faculty Interviews Administrative Analysis." Paper presented at the Tenth Annual Conference of Academic Chairpersons, February, Orlando, Florida.

Perry, W.L. 1993. "Preparing the Teaching Portfolio: A First Report." In *Successful Use of Teaching Portfolios,* edited by P. Seldin and Associates. Bolton, Mass.: Anker Publishing Co.

Rhem, J. 1991. "On the Road with Russell Edgerton." *National Teaching Learning Forum* 1: 1–2. ED 348 932. 74 pp. MF–01; PC–03.

———. 1994. "TQM by Another Name." *National Teaching Learning Forum* 36: 7.

Rice, R.E., and A.E. Austin. 1990. "Organizational Impacts on Faculty Morale and Motivation to Teach." In *How Administrators Can Improve Teaching,* edited by P. Seldin and Associates. San Francisco: Jossey-Bass.

Robbins, S.P. 1989. *Organizational Behavior: Concepts, Controversies, Applications.* Englewood Cliffs, N.J.: Prentice-Hall.

Robinson, J. 1993. "Faculty Orientations toward Teaching: The Use of Teaching Portfolios for Evaluating and Improving University-level Instruction." Paper presented at an annual meeting of the American Educational Research Association, April, Atlanta, Georgia. ED 358 149. 22 pp. MF–01; PC–01.

Root, L.S. 1987. "Faculty Evaluation: Reliability of Peer Assessment of Research, Teaching, and Service." *Research in Higher Education* 26: 71–84.

Schoenfeld, C. December 1992. "Will New Era in Washington Mute Criticisms of Higher Education?" *Academic Leader* 1: 4–5.

Schuster, J.H. 1990. "The Need for Fresh Approaches to Faculty Renewal." In *Enhancing Faculty Careers,* by J.H. Schuster, A.W. Wheeler, and Associates. San Francisco: Jossey-Bass.

Seagren, A.T., J.W. Creswell, and D.W. Wheeler. 1993. *The Department Chair: New Roles, Responsibilities, and Challenges.* ASHE-ERIC Higher Education Report No. 1. Washington, D.C.: George Washington Univ., School of Education and Human Development. ED 363 164. 129 pp. MF–01; PC–06.

Seldin, P. 1989. "Using Student Feedback to Improve Teaching." In *The Department Chairperson's Role in Enhancing College Teaching,* edited by A.F. Lucas. New Directions for Teaching and Learning No. 37. San Francisco: Jossey-Bass.

———. 1991. *The Teaching Portfolio.* Bolton, Mass.: Anker Publishing Co.

———. Fall 1992. "An Update on the Teaching Portfolio." *Department Chair:* 14–15.

———. October 1993a. "How Colleges Evaluate Professors: 1983 versus 1993." *AAHE Bulletin:* 6–8+. ED 371 665. 197 pp. MF–01; PC–08.

———. 1993b. *Successful Use of Teaching Portfolios.* Bolton, Mass.: Anker Publishing Co.

————. 1995. "Using Teaching Portfolios for Improvement of Faculty Evaluation." Paper presented at the Twelfth Annual Conference of Academic Chairpersons, February, Orlando, Florida.

Seldin, P., and L. Annis. 1990. "The Teaching Portfolio." *Journal of Staff, Program, and Organizational Development* 8: 197–201.

————. 1991–92. "The Teaching Portfolio." *Teaching Excellence: Toward the Best in the Academy:* 32.

Shackelford, R. 1993. "A Roundtable Discussion of the Portfolio and Its Results." In *Successful Use of Teaching Portfolios,* edited by P. Seldin and Associates. Bolton, Mass.: Anker Publishing Co.

Shelton, W.E., and D. DeZure. 1993. "Fostering a Teaching Culture in Higher Education." *Thought and Action* 8: 27–48.

Sherman, T.M., L.P. Armistead, F. Fowler, M.A Barksdale, and G. Reif. 1987. "The Quest for Excellence in University Teaching." *Journal of Higher Education* 48: 66–84.

Shore, B.M., et al. 1986. *The Teaching Dossier: A Guide to Its Preparation and Use.* Rev. ed. Montreal: Canadian Association of University Teachers.

Shulman, G.M., and J. Rhodes. 1995. "Assessing the Teaching-Learning Process: Using Portfolios for Empowerment." Paper presented at the Twelfth Annual Conference of Academic Chairpersons, February, Orlando, Florida.

Shulman, L.S. 1993. "Teaching as Community Property: Putting an End to Pedagogical Solitude." *Change* 25: 6–7.

Smith, K.S., and R.D. Simpson. 1995. "Validating Teaching Competencies for Faculty Members in Higher Education: A National Study Using the Delphi Method." *Innovative Higher Education* 19: 223–34.

Sorenson, D.L. 1994. "Valuing the Student Voice: Student Observer/Consultant Programs." *To Improve the Academy* 13: 97–108.

Stevens, E. 1988. "Tinkering with Teaching." *Review of Higher Education* 12: 63–78.

Stevens, J.J., and L.M. Aleamoni. 1985. "The Use of Evaluative Feedback for Instructional Improvement: A Longitudinal Perspective." *Instructional Science* 13: 285–304.

Stevenson, J.M. 1995. "Administrative Leadership to Support Teaching." *College Teaching* 43: 2.

"The Teaching Portfolio: Process and Product." 1994. In *Teaching.* Buffalo: SUNY College at Buffalo.

"Thoughts from the First Forum on Faculty Roles and Rewards." 1993. *Change* 25: 18–20.

Tierney, W.G., and R.A. Rhoads. 1993. *Enhancing Promotion, Tenure, and Beyond: Faculty Socialization as a Cultural Process.* ASHE-ERIC Higher Education Report No. 6. Washington, D.C.: George Washington Univ., School of Education and

Human Development. ED 368 322. 123 pp. MF–01; PC–05.

Urbach, F. 1992. "Developing a Teaching Portfolio." *College Teaching* 40: 71–74.

"Use of Faculty Portfolios Growing." July 1993. *Academic Leader:* 4.

Vroom, V.H., and A.G. Jago. 1988. *The New Leadership: Managing Participation in Organizations.* Englewood Cliffs, N.J.: Prentice-Hall.

Weimer, M. 1990. *Improving College Teaching: Strategies for Developing Instructional Effectiveness.* San Francisco: Jossey-Bass.

Weimer, M., J.L. Parrett, and M.M. Kerns. 1988. *How Am I Teaching?* Madison, Wisc.: Magna Publications.

Whetten, D.A., and K.S. Whetten. 1985. "Administrative Effectiveness in Higher Education." *Review of Higher Education* 9: 35–49.

Whitman, N., and E. Weiss. 1982. *Faculty Evaluation: The Use of Explicit Criteria for Promotion, Retention, and Tenure.* AAHE-ERIC Higher Education Research Report No. 2. Washington, D.C.: American Association for Higher Education. ED 221 148. 57 pp. MF–01; PC–Out of Print.

Wolf, K. October 1991. "The Schoolteacher's Portfolio: Issues in Design, Implementation, and Evaluation." *Phi Delta Kappan:* 129–36.

Zlotkowski, E. Summer 1996. "Service-Learning: Challenges and Opportunities for the Department Chair." *Department Chair: A Newsletter for Academic Administrators:* 3–5.

Zubizarreta, J. 1995. "How Teaching Portfolios Improve Course Instruction." Paper presented at the Lilly Conference on Excellence in College and University Teaching, June, Columbia, South Carolina.

INDEX

A

Activities to Improve Instruction as items for possible inclusion in a teaching portfolio, 30-31

administrators importance in introduction of teaching portfolios, 80-81

Annotated Course Materials as items for possible inclusion in a teaching portfolio, 30

assessing teaching

    colleagues as primary sources for, 57-60

    effectiveness as item for inclusion in a teaching portfolio, 25

    four primary sources for, 49

    self as primary sources for, 56-57

    students as primary sources for, 50-56

atmosphere of collegiality

   importance in promoting excellence in teaching, 95

"atmospheric guidance," 90

B

Boyer, Ernest (1990)

   Scholarship Reconsidered: The Priorities of the Professorate , x

Brigham Young University, 55-56

Brinko, K. T. (1993)

   18-item multiple-choice survey form, 53

bubble-up theory, 90

C

changing the reward structure to emphasize teaching, 76-78

Chickering and Gamson (1967)

    statements of personal convictions, 64

collaborative approach to teaching evaluation, 58-59

colleagues

    as primary sources for assessing teaching, 57-60

    can reliably evaluate checklist, 58

    danger of evaluation of, 58

collegiality

    importance of, 88

Commission of Inquiry on Canadian University Education, 73

Committee C of the AAUP, 72

"community property"

    teaching must become, 95

    teaching will never achieve deserved status until it becomes, 61

Competencies Required for Good Teachers, 66-67

content of a teaching portfolio, 22-24
Continuous Quality Improvement
        creative format for eliciting students' opinion on instruction, 54
Contributions to Institution or Profession as items for possible inclusion in a teaching portfolio, 30-31
Core Characteristics for Excellent Teachers, 68-69
Course
        Materials as items for possible inclusion in a portfolio, 30
        syllabus as an evaluation criteria, 41
CQI. See Continuous Quality Improvement
"crisis in spirit," 42
criteria in developing standards to evaluate teaching portfolios, 37
criticisms of professors
        validity of, 1

D

Delphi technique, 64
department chairs as key players, 85-86
difficult faculty
        dealing with, 98-99
dimensions as organizing principles for a teaching portfolio, 21-22
Documentation for possible inclusion in a teaching portfolio of
        Students' Learning, 30
        teaching strategies, 24
documenting teaching, 9
drawbacks in definition of good teaching, 64

E

effectiveness of portfolio items for improvement of teaching, 23
effective teachers
        student identified eight characteristics of, 65
effective teaching
        departmental characteristics of, 87
e-mail
        use to obtain student evaluations, 55
ethnographic or qualitative studies of teaching, 65-70
evaluation committees
        key questions that should ask, 40
evaluation
        criteria for a teaching portfolio, 39-43
        of Teaching for possible inclusion in a teaching portfolio, 30-31

excellent departments
  characteristics of, 86-88
exercises to start a teaching portfolio, 34-35
explicit criteria for evaluation
  undesirable results from the use of, 42

F

faculty development program
  need to establish respected, 83
faculty visitation of classrooms requires structure, 60
fairness of
  trustworthy evidence evaluation, 47
"Faux Student" as student observer role, 56
Filmmaker as student observer role, 56
fit between potential candidate and department, 97
"formative evaluation," 49
Frost, Peter
  supporter of research over teaching, 74
Fuhrmann and Grasha (1983)
  provide forms aimed at different aspects of teaching, 52-53

G

"gatekeepers" function in promoting teaching, 96
goals
  assessment form, 53
  the setting of, 93-94
"good talk about good teaching" need to create, 95
good teaching or effective teaching
  current state of knowledge about, 63-70
  definition depends on the purpose, 61
  need for definition of, 102
  types of literature on, 63
graduate students
  importance of training how to teach, 81-82
Grasha, Dr. Anthony F., xi

H

H. G. Murray (1987)
  60-item diagnostic instrument of, 52
"hidden characteristics" of community college teachers, 68
hiring new faculty, 97-98
Honors or Recognition as items for possible inclusion in a teaching
  portfolio, 30-31

I

information from others as item for possible inclusion in a teaching
      portfolio, 26-28
"informative feedback." See "formative evaluation"
in-house visiting lecturers, 93
insanity, perfect example of, ix
instructional methods and content are discipline-specific, 62
internal sabbatical leave, 93
Interviewer as student observer role, 56
items for possible inclusion in a Teaching Portfolio, 24-28, 30-31

K

Kennedy, Donald
      central administrators relatively powerless to effect change,
      6
key to transformation of a department, 90
knowledge of discipline as necessary but not sufficient condition
      for
      successful teaching, 3

L

The law of legitimate measurement, ix
The law of reward and appreciation, ix
The law of survival, ix
The law of value, ix
learning, more than improving teaching technique, important, 62-
      63
Leggett, William
      research keeps universities intellectually healthy, 74-75
legislation regulating faculty workloads enacted by 21 states, 1
list of "core characteristics" that define excellent teachers at
      Miami-Dade Community College, 65

M

McGill University, 74-75
Master Faculty program, 59-60
material from oneself for inclusion in a teaching portfolio, 26
materials as an organizing principles for a teaching portfolio, 21-22
merit pay as a disincentive, 91-92
Miami-Dade Community College
      core characteristics for excellent teachers at, 68-69
      list of "core characteristics" defining excellent teachers at,
      65

Miller (1987)
> offers short form for student appraisal of classroom teaching, 53

mission statement, 89

Murray, Dr. Judy I., xi

Murray, J. P. (1991) description of SGID like technique
> that can be used without a facilitator, 53

myths embedded in culture of higher education, 3

myth that good or effective teaching cannot be defined precisely
> enough to be evaluated, 38

N

National Survey of Postsecondary Faculty for 1987-88, 73

O

Old Dominion University
> unsuccessful attempt to introduce teaching portfolios at, 82

P

Pacheco, President Manuel T.
> research dollars pay for undergraduate equipment, 74

paid student observers, 55-56

Palmer, P. J. (1993)
> "good talk about good teaching" need, 95

parking as a teaching incentive, 92-93

"pedagogy of substance, 4

philosophy of education, 24-25, 28-29

philosophy of teaching as key component of portfolio, 34-35

portfolio readers
> training of, 43-44
> value of a highly trained group of, 43

"Primed Student" as student observer role, 56

process of change
> steps in, 89

products of good teaching as item for possible inclusion in a
> teaching portfolio, 26

professors ill-trained to be teachers, 2

Q

qualitative material
> use in making decisions about personnel, 38

qualitative studies
> drawbacks in definition of good teaching, 64

steps taken to evaluate and improve ones teaching as
       item for possible inclusion in a teaching portfolio, 26-27
Student Consultant as student observer role, 56
student identified eight characteristics of effective teachers, 65
students as primary sources for assessing teaching, 50-56
successful teachers
       characteristics that led a few to be, 69-70
"sudden death implications" of formative evaluation techniques, 50
"summative evaluation," 49
SUNY system
       effect of lack of leadership in, 1
Syracuse University
       teaching graduate students how to teach at, 82

T

TABS. See Teaching Analysis by Students
teaching
       need to discuss, 95-96
Teaching Analysis by Students, 50
       history of development and value of, 52
teaching
       award leads to temporary salary increase and drastic salary
         reduction at University of North Carolina at Chapel Hill,
       75
       can't get you tenure but bad teaching can get you fired, 77
       "doesn't count" message, 73
       improvement plan as item for possible inclusion in a
       portfolio, 25
teaching portfolio
       ability to illustrate what is best about a professor's teaching,
       10
       advantages that bring to higher education, 76-77
       can result in several outcomes, 14-15
       defining by purpose, 9
       demonstrates teaching as an institutional priority, 11-12
       empowerment of professors through, 10-11
       essential in assessing teaching and improving learning, 76
       individualizes faculty development, 12-14
       necessary conditions for, 78-83
       need to specify minimum content of, 101
       organizing principles of, 20-24
       reason for, 14-15

should contain statement of the philosophy of teaching, 101

standards that must conform to, 19

strategies and philosophy, match between, 32

takes into consideration fundamental laws of human behavior, x

too risky except in supportive collegial environment, 79

uses from perspective of faculty member, 15-16

uses of, 101

value, 76-77

teaching strategies and reflection

documentation of, 32-33

techniques for formative evaluation by students, 50

theme as organizing principle of teaching portfolio, 20

Total Quality Management creative format for

eliciting students' opinion on how to improve instruction, 54

TQM. See Total Quality Management

"transformational leadership," 89

triangulation strategy, 47

trustworthy evidence evaluation

fairness of, 47

reliability of, 44-46

requires thoughtful selection of raters, 45

social consequences of, 47-48

for teaching portfolios, 44-48

U

University of Arizona, 72, 74

University of British Columbia, 74

University of California system survey, 72

University of Chicago, 59

University of Cincinnati, xi

University of Massachusetts at Amherst, 52

University of North Carolina at Chapel Hill, 75

University of Washington, 52

U.S. House Committee on Children, Youth, and Families, 1

V

validity of trustworthy evidence evaluation, 46

vision as the means by which a chair can create a focus or agenda for the department's plans, 90

W

what is taught as item for possible inclusion in a teaching
        portfolio, 24
who is taught for possible inclusion in a teaching portfolio, 24
why they are taught for possible inclusion in teaching portfolio, 24
"wisdom of practice," 4

ASHE-ERIC HIGHER EDUCATION REPORTS

Since 1983, the Association for the Study of Higher Education (ASHE) and the Educational Resources Information Center (ERIC) Clearinghouse on Higher Education, a sponsored project of the Graduate School of Education and Human Development at The George Washington University, have cosponsored the ASHE-ERIC Higher Education Report series. The 1995 series is the twenty-fourth overall and the seventh to be published by the Graduate School of Education and Human Development at The George Washington University.

Each monograph is the definitive analysis of a tough higher education problem, based on thorough research of pertinent literature and institutional experiences. Topics are identified by a national survey. Noted practitioners and scholars are then commissioned to write the reports, with experts providing critical reviews of each manuscript before publication.

Eight monographs (10 before 1985) in the ASHE-ERIC Higher Education Report series are published each year and are available on individual and subscription bases. To order, use the order form on the last page of this book.

Qualified persons interested in writing a monograph for the ASHE-ERIC Higher Education Report series are invited to submit a proposal to the National Advisory Board. As the preeminent literature review and issue analysis series in higher education, the Higher Education Reports are guaranteed wide dissemination and national exposure for accepted candidates. Execution of a monograph requires at least a minimal familiarity with the ERIC database, including *Resources in Education* and the current *Index to Journals in Education*. The objective of these reports is to bridge conventional wisdom with practical research. Prospective authors are strongly encouraged to call Dr. Fife at 800-773-3742.

For further information, write to
    ASHE-ERIC Higher Education Reports
    The George Washington University
    One Dupont Circle, Suite 630
    Washington, DC 20036
Or phone (202) 296-2597; toll free: 800-773-ERIC.

Write or call for a complete catalog.

ADVISORY BOARD

James Earl Davis
University of Delaware at Newark

Susan Frost
Emory University

Mildred Garcia
Montclair State College

James Hearn
University of Georgia

Bruce Anthony Jones
University of Pittsburgh

L. Jackson Newell
Deep Springs College

Carolyn Thompson
State University of New York–Buffalo

Steven G. Olswang
University of Washington

Sherry Sayles-Folks
Eastern Michigan University

Karl Schilling
Miami University

Pamela D. Sherer
The Center for Teaching Excellence

Lawrence A. Sherr
University of Kansas

Marilla D. Svinicki
University of Texas–Austin

David Sweet
OERI, U.S. Department of Education

Kathe Taylor
State of Washington Higher Education Coordinating Board

W. Allan Wright
Dalhousle University

Donald H. Wulff
University of Washington

Manta Yorke
Liverpool John Moores University

REVIEW PANEL

Charles Adams
University of Massachusetts–Amherst

Louis Albert
American Association for Higher Education

Richard Alfred
University of Michigan

Henry Lee Allen
University of Rochester

Philip G. Altbach
Boston College

Marilyn J. Amey
University of Kansas

Kristine L. Anderson
Florida Atlantic University

Karen D. Arnold
Boston College

Robert J. Barak
Iowa State Board of Regents

Alan Bayer
Virginia Polytechnic Institute and State University

John P. Bean
Indiana University–Bloomington

John M. Braxton
Peabody College, Vanderbilt University

Ellen M. Brier
Tennessee State University

Barbara E. Brittingham
The University of Rhode Island

Dennis Brown
University of Kansas

Peter McE. Buchanan
Council for Advancement and Support of Education

Patricia Carter
University of Michigan

John A. Centra
Syracuse University

Arthur W. Chickering
George Mason University

Darrel A. Clowes
Virginia Polytechnic Institute and State University

Cynthia S. Dickens
Mississippi State University

Deborah M. DiCroce
Piedmont Virginia Community College

Sarah M. Dinham
University of Arizona

Kenneth A. Feldman
State University of New York–Stony Brook

Dorothy E. Finnegan
The College of William & Mary

Mildred Garcia
Montclair State College

Rodolfo Z. Garcia
Commission on Institutions of Higher Education

Kenneth C. Green
University of Southern California

James Hearn
University of Georgia

Edward R. Hines
Illinois State University

Deborah Hunter
University of Vermont

Philo Hutcheson
Georgia State University

Bruce Anthony Jones
University of Pittsburgh

Elizabeth A. Jones
The Pennsylvania State University

Kathryn Kretschmer
University of Kansas

Marsha V. Krotseng
State College and University Systems of West Virginia

George D. Kuh
Indiana University–Bloomington

Daniel T. Layzell
University of Wisconsin System

Patrick G. Love
Kent State University

Cheryl D. Lovell
State Higher Education Executive Officers

Meredith Jane Ludwig
American Association of State Colleges and Universities

Dewayne Matthews
Western Interstate Commission for Higher Education

Mantha V. Mehallis
Florida Atlantic University

Toby Milton
Essex Community College

James R. Mingle
State Higher Education Executive Officers

John A. Muffo
Virginia Polytechnic Institute and State University

L. Jackson Newell
Deep Springs College

James C. Palmer
Illinois State University

Robert A. Rhoads
The Pennsylvania State University

G. Jeremiah Ryan
Harford Community College

Mary Ann Danowitz Sagaria
The Ohio State University

Daryl G. Smith
The Claremont Graduate School

William G. Tierney
University of Southern California

Susan B. Twombly
University of Kansas

Robert A. Walhaus
University of Illinois–Chicago

Harold Wechsler
University of Rochester

Elizabeth J. Whitt
University of Illinois–Chicago

Michael J. Worth
The George Washington University

RECENT TITLES

1995 ASHE-ERIC Higher Education Reports

1. Tenure, Promotion, and Reappointment: Legal and Administrative Implications
   Benjamin Baez and John A. Centra

2. Taking Teaching Seriously: Meeting the Challenge of Instructional Improvement
   Michael B. Paulsen and Kenneth A. Feldman

3. Empowering the Faculty: Mentoring Redirected and Renewed
   Gaye Luna and Deborah L. Cullen

4. Enhancing Student Learning: Intellectual, Social, and Emotional Integration
   Anne Goodsell Love and Patrick G. Love

5. Benchmarking in Higher Education: Adapting Best Practices to Improve Quality
   Jeffrey W. Alstete

6. Models for Improving College Teaching: A Faculty Resource
   Jon E. Travis

7. Experiential Learning in Higher Education: Linking Classroom and Community
   Jeffrey A. Cantor

1994 ASHE-ERIC Higher Education Reports

1. The Advisory Committee Advantage: Creating an Effective Strategy for Programmatic Improvement
   Lee Teitel

2. Collaborative Peer Review: The Role of Faculty in Improving College Teaching
   Larry Keig and Michael D. Waggoner

3. Prices, Productivity, and Investment: Assessing Financial Strategies in Higher Education
   Edward P. St. John

4. The Development Officer in Higher Education: Toward an Understanding of the Role
   Michael J. Worth and James W. Asp II

5. Measuring Up: The Promises and Pitfalls of Performance Indicators in Higher Education
   Gerald Gaither, Brian P. Nedwek, and John E. Neal

6. A New Alliance: Continuous Quality and Classroom Effectiveness
   Mimi Wolverton

7. Redesigning Higher Education: Producing Dramatic Gains in Student Learning
   Lion F. Gardiner

---

8. Student Learning outside the Classroom: Transcending Artificial Boundaries
   George D. Kuh, Katie Branch Douglas, Jon P. Lund, and Jackie Ramin-Gyurnek

1993 ASHE-ERIC Higher Education Reports

1. The Department Chair: New Roles, Responsibilities, and Challenges
   Alan T. Seagren, John W. Creswell, and Daniel W. Wheeler

2. Sexual Harassment in Higher Education: From Conflict to Community
   Robert O. Riggs, Patricia H. Murrell, and JoAnne C. Cutting

3. Chicanos in Higher Education: Issues and Dilemmas for the 21st Century
   Adalberto Aguirre, Jr., and Ruben O. Martinez

4. Academic Freedom in American Higher Education: Rights, Responsibilities, and Limitations
   Robert K. Poch

5. Making Sense of the Dollars: The Costs and Uses of Faculty Compensation
   Kathryn M. Moore and Marilyn J. Amey

6. Enhancing Promotion, Tenure, and Beyond: Faculty Socialization as a Cultural Process
   William G. Tierney and Robert A. Rhoads

7. New Perspectives for Student Affairs Professionals: Evolving Realities, Responsibilities, and Roles
   Peter H. Garland and Thomas W. Grace

8. Turning Teaching into Learning: The Role of Student Responsibility in the Collegiate Experience
   Todd M. Davis and Patricia Hillman Murrell

1992 ASHE-ERIC Higher Education Reports

1. The Leadership Compass: Values and Ethics in Higher Education
   John R. Wilcox and Susan L. Ebbs

2. Preparing for a Global Community: Achieving an International Perspective in Higher Education
   Sarah M. Pickert

3. Quality: Transforming Postsecondary Education
   Ellen Earle Chaffee and Lawrence A. Sherr

4. Faculty Job Satisfaction: Women and Minorities in Peril
   Martha Wingard Tack and Carol Logan Patitu

5. Reconciling Rights and Responsibilities of Colleges and Students: Offensive Speech, Assembly, Drug Testing, and Safety
   Annette Gibbs

6. Creating Distinctiveness: Lessons from Uncommon Colleges and Universities
   Barbara K. Townsend, L. Jackson Newell, and Michael D. Wiese

7. Instituting Enduring Innovations: Achieving Continuity of Change in Higher Education
   Barbara K. Curry

8. Crossing Pedagogical Oceans: International Teaching Assistants in U.S. Undergraduate Education
   Rosslyn M. Smith, Patricia Byrd, Gayle L. Nelson, Ralph Pat Barrett, and Janet C. Constantinides

1991 ASHE-ERIC Higher Education Reports

1. Active Learning: Creating Excitement in the Classroom
   Charles C. Bonwell and James A. Eison

2. Realizing Gender Equality in Higher Education: The Need to Integrate Work/Family Issues
   Nancy Hensel

3. Academic Advising for Student Success: A System of Shared Responsibility
   Susan H. Frost

4. Cooperative Learning: Increasing College Faculty Instructional Productivity
   David W. Johnson, Roger T. Johnson, and Karl A. Smith

5. High School–College Partnerships: Conceptual Models, Programs, and Issues
   Arthur Richard Greenberg

6. Meeting the Mandate: Renewing the College and Departmental Curriculum
   William Toombs and William G. Tierney

7. Faculty Collaboration: Enhancing the Quality of Scholarship and Teaching
   Ann E. Austin and Roger G. Baldwin

8. Strategies and Consequences: Managing the Costs in Higher Education
   John S. Waggaman

_____ Please begin my subscription to the 1996 *ASHE-ERIC Higher Education Reports* (Volume 25) at $98.00, 31% off the cover price, starting with Report 1, 1996. Includes shipping. _____

_____ Please send a complete set of the 1995 *ASHE-ERIC Higher Education Reports* at $98.00, 31% off the cover price. Please add shipping charge below. _____

Individual reports are available at the following prices:
1993, 1994, 1995, and 1996 (Volume 25) $18.00; 1988–1992, $17.00; 1980–1987, $15.00

SHIPPING CHARGES
For orders of more than 50 books, please call for shipping information.

	1st three books	*Ea. addl. book*
U.S., 48 Contiguous States		
Ground:	$3.75	$0.15
2nd Day*:	8.25	1.10
Next Day*:	18.00	1.60
Alaska & Hawaii (2nd Day Only)*:	13.25	1.40

U.S. Territories and Foreign Countries: Please call for shipping information.
*Order will be shipped within 24 hours of request.
All prices shown on this form are subject to change.

PLEASE SEND ME THE FOLLOWING REPORTS:

Quantity	Report No.	Year	Title	Amount

Please check one of the following:
☐ Check enclosed, payable to GWU-ERIC.
☐ Purchase order attached.
☐ Charge my credit card indicated below:
  ☐ Visa   ☐ MasterCard

Subtotal: _____
Shipping: _____
Total Due: _____

Expiration Date_____

Name_____

Title_____

Institution _____

Address_____

City _____ State _____ Zip_____

Phone _____ Fax _____Telex_____

Signature _____ Date_____

SEND ALL ORDERS TO: ASHE-ERIC Higher Education Reports
The George Washington University
One Dupont Cir., Ste. 630, Washington, DC 20036-1183
Phone: (202) 296-2597 • Toll-free: 800-773-ERIC